ALCESTIS BARCINONENSIS

MNEMOSYNE

BIBLIOTHECA CLASSICA BATAVA

COLLEGERUNT

A. D. LEEMAN · H. W. PLEKET · C. J. RUIJGH

BIBLIOTHECAE FASCISULOS EDENDOS CURAVIT

C. J. RUIJGH, KLASSIEK SEMINARIUM, OUDE TURFMARKT 129, AMSTERDAM

SUPPLEMENTUM CENTESIMUM TERTIUM

MIROSLAV MARCOVICH

ALCESTIS BARCINONENSIS

ALCESTIS BARCINONENSIS

TEXT AND COMMENTARY

BY

MIROSLAV MARCOVICH

E. J. BRILL

LEIDEN • NEW YORK • KØBENHAVN • KÖLN
1988

Library of Congress Cataloging
lc number 87-37212

PA
6140
.A420
1988

ISSN   0169-8958
ISBN   90 04 08600 5

PRINTED IN THE NETHERLANDS BY E. J. BRILL

IOANNI L. HELLER
<small>Octogenario</small>
DDD

CONTENTS

INTRODUCTION

A) *The Text*

The P. Barcinonensis Inv. Nos. 158ab, 159ab, 160ab, and 161a consists of four leaves (125 × 103 mm), which were later incorporated into a *codex mixtus* as its fols. 33-36. The codex is the property of the Foundation Sant Lluc Evangelista at Barcelona. The papyrus comprises a fascinating late Latin poem of 122 hexameters (the original poem probably had at least 124 lines) dealing with the heroic death of Alcestis to save the life of her beloved husband Admetus. The text of the poem spreads over six closely written pages of the papyrus, with four lines on the seventh page.

The script is early half-uncial with cursive elements, most probably belonging to the second half of the fourth century A.D. Our *Alcestis* is preceded in the Barcelona codex by Cicero's *Catilinarians* 1 and 2 (fols. 1-24a); by a Latin *Psalmus Responsorius* (fols. 24b-28a); and by a Greek liturgical text (fols. 29b-32). New surprises may be expected from the rest of the folios. Probable provenance of the codex is Egypt.[1]

Dr. R. Roca-Puig from Barcelona deserves the gratitude of scholars for publishing first the Barcelona *Psalm* (Barcelona, 1965), then the *Catilinarians* 1 and 2 (Barcelona, 1977), and now *Alcestis* as well.[2] He has provided us with an accurate transcript of the papyrus, along with reasonably clear photographs. His attempt at the restoration of the original poem, however, was far from being satisfactory.

The papyrus is preserved in relatively good physical condition; the patches with poor quality of material (e.g., on p. 158a) are minimal. The text of the poem has been copied in a readable hand, as if it were prose, all in one breath. What makes the text difficult to read and understand is primarily its scribe. Doubtless, he was copying from a poor exemplar, plagued with textual corruptions, lacunae, and intrusive marginal glosses. For example, in v. 1 there is a supralinear gloss *apollo* explaining the rare epithet *lauripotens*. But in v. 3, the same supralinear gloss *apollo* had ousted the original reading of the poem (probably, *arcitenens*).

---

[1] The five papyrus leaves containing *Psalmus Responsorius* are briefly described by E. A. Lowe, as No. 1782 of the *Supplement* to his *Codices Latini Antiquiores* (Oxford, 1971, p. 32). Lowe dated the script of the Psalm to "saec. IV[2]." The same will be true of the script of our *Alcestis*, since it is copied by the same scribe.

[2] R. Roca-Puig, *Alcestis. Hexàmetres Llatins*. Papyri Barcinonenses, Inv. n. 158-161 (Barcelona, 1982) = *Ed.*

Intrusive marginal indications are present, e.g., in vv. 13 and 72: *apollo inquit* and *alcestis inquit*, respectively (and there are several marginal indications of the speaker in the papyrus). Finally, there is a blank space in line 124.

The main culprit, however, is the scribe. He proves to be exceptionally illiterate and negligent. Lowe's remark on the text of the *Psalm* remains valid for the text of *Alcestis* as well: "... the scribe was unused to copying Latin." "... by a scribe who did not quite understand what he was copying." P. J. Parsons shares this view: "Everything suggests an uncomprehending scribe with a difficult exemplar: the copy abounds in elementary errors and serious corruptions."

There may be more to it than this. First, our scribe apparently knew the spoken Vulgar Latin, but not enough of the classical Latin of the poem he was copying. Both the phonology and morphology of his text seem to reflect a struggle between a vulgar and a classical form. Consider a few examples:

    5   me (for mi); 24 requeret (for requirit); 61 fratre (for fratri<s>); 67
        perdedit *bis*; 68 etin (for Ityn); 76 m<or>eor and 96 moreor; 123
        rapeor; 124 claudet (for claudit)
    9   famolum; 11 iossi (for iussi); 39 tomul<i>; 72 sepolcris; 89 titolum
   10   post crimine; 76 post funere nostro
   12   fatebo (for fatebo<r>); 91 desere (for desera<r>)
   13   mors uicinam
   26   and 29 genitur (for genitor); 52 murari (for morari); 55 urbis (for
        orbis); 112 odures (for odores); 112 crucum (for crocum)
   27   nufas (for nefas); 39 contustant (for cont<r>istant); 78 trustior (for
        tristior); 100 dissimiles (for dissimuler)
   30   tumulis (for tumulos); 119 oculos (for oculis)
   41   tumulus (for tumulos); 59 locus (for locos); 78 atrus (for atros); 110
        pictus (for pictos); 116 arsurus (for arsuros)
   41   ed (for et); 50 consumad; 55 adque (for atque); 72 inquid (for inquit)
   43   dante (for ante)
   45   nec pietatem... uincitur
   45   fletus (for fletu); 118 manos (for manu)
   47   materna cernere morte
   48   ubira (for ubera); similarly, 40 uellis (for velles); 52 possis (for
        posses); 104 alis (for ales)
   49   deripiat (for diripia<n>t); 116 desponit, but 113 and 115 distringit
        (for destringit)
   84   uestigiam ne mea... tegat
   89   unguentum (for unguento), but 121 in gremio refugit
  117   ratura (for ra<p>tura)
  124   sembra soporem (for membra sopore)

And second, some of the scribal errors seem to reflect a *deliberate* effort, on the part of the scribe, to correct his exemplar. Consider these examples of a possible or probable improvisation:

1   doli piant (for Deli<e> P<a>ean)
2   tuus (for tuo); 31 tuo (for tuam); 41 tuo (for tibi)
5   relinqua[[nt]]m (for relinquant) and 80 recedam (for recedat)
7   uita futuri (for vita futura)
9   si {non} te colui
13 premit mestum (for premit maesti)
15 subiret (for subire)
24 lacrimarum causa (for lacrimis <quae> causa)
25 fatorum damna sororum (for fatorum damna suorum), under the
    influence of 4 fatalia fila sorores
26 ecce uides (for ecce, dies)
33 gratamque manum (for grateque manum)
36 and 40 nihil (for nil)
36 sicut suum (for si quod sum)
37 uitae meae (for vita meae)
39 dulcior ullam (for dulcius una) [cf. 84 dulcior ulla]
50 meae lucis (for mihi lucis)
52 aeternam sede (for ter<r>ena <in> sede)
55 adque [i.e., atque] (for ac)
61 stygium regnum (for Stygii regnum)
61 multatus (for mutatus)
66 diomedes (for Diomede) and acatem [i.e., Achatem] (for Agaue)
67 ion (for Ino)
68 illa cruentus (for ilia cruda)
69 precedunt (for cedunt)
81 me tradere pulcris (for me trade sepulcris)
87 neue digna retinere (for {neve} dignare tenere)
90 {sub nocte}, under the influence of 86 tecum sub nocte iacere
97 tibi (for mihi)
114 puluer amoni (for pulver amomum)

As a consequence, the papyrus poses major problems for reading and interpreting the poem. After its publication (18 October 1982), four attempts at recovering the original poem were made at the same time (in 1983) but independently of each other: one by W. D. Lebek, another by a team of Oxford scholars (P. J. Parsons, R. G. M. Nisbet, G. O. Hutchinson), a third one by myself, and a fourth one by V. Tandoi. The result of this combined effort is the following reconstruction of the original poem.

In many places, the text still remains tentative only. Nevertheless, I am confident that the general content of the poem is clear enough to allow an attempt at its interpretation and the assessment of the probable sources of inspiration for the Barcelona bard.[3]

---

[3] Previous scholarship on the poem: *Ed.* (note 2); W. D. Lebek, *ZPE* 52 (1983) 1-29; P. J. Parsons, R. G. M. Nisbet, G. O. Hutchinson, *ibidem*, 31-36; M. Marcovich, ZAnt 33 (1983) 119-28; Idem, *ICS* 9 (1984) 111-34; Idem, in *Apophoreta Philologica Emmanueli Fernández-Galiano Oblata*, II (Mantuae Carpetanorum, 1984) 283-95; Idem, *ZPE* 65 (1986)

B)The Poem

(1) *Literary Genre.* Formally speaking, the Barcelona *Alcestis* belongs to
the literary genre of late Latin exercises in verse composition, rhetoric,
mythological erudition, and—above all—*ethopoeia* of a hero or a heroine.
As closest parallels come to mind the *Alcesta* (162 hexameters long) of the
Latin Anthology (I, No. 15 Riese), and Dracontius' *Hylas* (163 hexameters:
Romulea II, ed. Fr. Vollmer: *M.G.H.* XIV). But what a difference
between the *Alcesta* and the new *Alcestis*! The former is one hundred per-
cent a Vergilian cento[4]: the latter is an original poem, the product of a
reasonably gifted, skilled and learned poet. To quote only the Oxonienses (*ZPE* 52 [1983] 31), the *Alcesta* of *A.L.* is "a flaccid pastiche
which points up the merits of the Barcelona bard."

Our poet is building upon the best traditions of Latin poetry; his diction shows unmistakable borrowings from Lucretius, Vergil, Horace,
Propertius, Ovid, Silius Italicus, Lucan, Statius, and many others. His
metrics are correct, his colometry is convincing enough when dealing
with a late Latin poet. The flow of words is natural and attests to the fact
that the Barcelona poet had succeeded in producing a fluent, lively and
enjoyable Latin.

There is, however, much more to it than simply style and diction. Our
poet proves to be a rather ambitious, sophisticated, and well-versed *poeta
doctus*, by displaying a carefully conceived *design*, innovation in his treatment of the traditional Alcestis-myth, a vivid imagination, in addition to
mythological and folkloric erudition, as I shall try to demonstrate in the
Commentary.

(2) *Structure.* The *Alcestis* consists of *twelve* blocks (or passages), varying
in size from seven to thirteen lines. In this edition, each block is printed
on a separate page. Now, the poem easily falls into the following five
parts:

A. The dialogue between Admetus and Apollo (1-20)   [2 blocks]
B. The dialogue between Admetus and Pheres (21-42)   [2 blocks]
        The *Agon* between Clymene and Alcestis:
C. Clymene's *rhesis* (42-70)   [3 blocks]

39-57; 69 (1987) 231-36; V. Tandoi, *Anonymi Carmen de Alcestide nuper repertum* (Foggia,
Atlantica Editrice, 1984) 1-11.

Textual Criticism: J. Diggle, *ZPE* 54 (1984) 36; W. S. Watt, *ibidem*, 37 f.; R. Führer,
ibidem, 39; D. R. Shackleton Bailey, *ZPE* 55 (1984) 1 f.

Interpretation: J. Schwartz, *ZPE* 52 (1983) 37-39; Chr. Schäublin, *MH* 41 (1984) 174-
81; A. Garzya, Κοινωνία (Naples) 9 (1985) 7-14; G. Harrison, D. Obbink, *ZPE* 63 (1986)
75-81.

[4] Compare now David F. Bright, "Theory and Practice in the Vergilian Cento", *ICS*
9 (1984) 79-90, Table on p. 85.

D. Alcestis' *anti-rhesis* (71-103)   [3 blocks]

E. The last day and death of the heroine (104-124)   [2 blocks]

With the exception of the obvious lacunae between lines 101 and 102, and between 110 and 111, I think the poem is preserved as complete: it opens with a grandiloquent invocation of Apollo; it closes with the death of the heroine (just as the *Alcesta* of *A.L.* does). Hutchinson believes, however, that the beginning and the end of the poem are missing. Now, each one of the twelve blocks of the poem is full of surprises for the reader, as we shall see both in this brief Introduction and in the Commentary.

(3) *The Characters: Admetus, Apollo, Pheres, Clymene, Alcestis. Admetus* is depicted by our poet as a foolish weakling. His lack of religious wisdom is reflected right at the opening of the poem. Starting from the premise that Apollo owes him a big favor (9-11: *si te colui...*, *succepi...*, *accepi iussi<que> idem...*), Admetus addresses Apollo (probably in Delphi) with this self-confident and arrogant request (3-6):

> ... da scire diem, da noscere, *quando*
> rumpant Admeti fatalia fila Sorores.
> 5   *Quae* finis vitae, *qui<d>* mi post fata relinquant,
> edoce, siderea<s> animus quando ivit in auras.

These three questions—*quando, quae finis vitae,* and *quid mi post*—reveal to us that Admetus wants to know what no mortal man is supposed to know, namely: the length of his life-span; the very cause of his death; and—above all—the future of his own *self* after the death. Apollo obliges, but not before rebuking Admetus for his hubristic request (12 f.): *Doleo, sed vera fatebo<r>: / mors vicina premit...*

As for Admetus' unmanly behavior, it is reflected, first, in his emotional outburst when talking to his father (29 f.: *tu, genitor, tu, sancte, potes: si tempora dones, / si pro me...*); second, in his pusillanimity with his mother (42 f.: *pulsus genetricis / volvitur ante pedes, vestigia blandus adorat...*); finally, in his "endless weeping" throughout the poem. It starts with 22 (*et fletibus atria conplet*) and 24 (*lacrimis <quae> causa*), to continue in 44 (*inque sinus fundit lacrimas*) and 45 (*fletu*), and to end with 71 (*coniugis ut talis vidit Peleïa fletus*) and 107 (*lacrimasq<ue> viri... videbat*).

No wonder then that the heroine felt her husband badly needed encouragement and moral instruction for his future marital life. Hence Alcestis' final injunction addressed to Admetus (102 f.): 'And you too, Admetus, learn to die for your (future) dear wife (if need be)...!'' (*Et tu pro coniuge cara / disce mori...*).

Apollo appears in the poem as a faithful servant of the supreme Fates. Notice the chain of command reflected in line 27 f.: *Hoc Parc<a>e* *docuere nefas, hoc noster Apollo / invitus, pater, edocuit.* There is nothing here of Apollo's bravado from Euripides' *Alcestis* 11 f.: παιδὸς Φέρητος, ὃν θανεῖν ἐρρυσάμην, / Μοίρας δολώσας. Apollo also remains a trusty member of Admetus' family (*noster Apollo*). Following the traditional myth (Eurip. *Alc.* 10 and 23; Hygin. *Fab.* 51.2; Stat. *Theb.* 6.377 f.), our poet makes Apollo feel grateful and attached to Admetus (12, *doleo*; 28, *invitus*). Still, he must fulfill his duty. Consequently, Apollo's message to Admetus is straightforward: (1) *Mors vicina premit* (13), and (2) Look for a substitute victim (a *victima vicaria*), coming from your own family (15-20). As was to expect, Apollo chooses to ignore Admetus' impertinent questions about (5) *quae finis vitae* and *qui<d> mi post fata relinquant.*

(4) *Pietas as the key-idea of the poem.* The character of Pheres, Clymene, and Alcestis depends on one single concept. For in the responses of Pheres (32-42), Clymene (42-70), and Alcestis (71-103) to Admetus' plight the pivotal role belongs to the concept of *pietas*, which I take to mean here, "the sense of duty of a family-member (or a φίλος)." In my view, *pietas* is the keyword of this *ethopoeia*. The word itself is repeated three times by the poet (45; 75; 103) for the benefit of the reader, in addition to the expressions, *coniux pia* (78), and, *matris pia... umbra* (99), both of them referring to the pious Alcestis.

The message of the poet seems to be clear enough. It is a sacred duty (*pietas*) for a loving family-member (father, mother, spouse, children) to give his/her life, in case of necessity, for a beloved member of the same family. In a marriage, this duty between the spouses is *reciprocal*. Hence Alcestis' motto: *pro coniuge coniux* (74). And for the same reason she chooses to close her *rhesis* with this moral addressed both to her husband and to any future married reader of this *ethopoeia* (102 f.): *Et tu pro coniuge cara / disce mori, de m<e> disce exemplu<m> pietatis.*

Now, neither Pheres nor Clymene possess this sense of family-duty (*pietas*). That is why the poet hastens to tell us that Pheres is "a father by name alone:" *Hic genitor, non ut genitor* (32), "Hear now the father speaking unlike a father," reflecting a πατὴρ ἀπάτωρ of Greek tragedy. As for Clymene, the poet is even more explicit (45): *nec pietate... vincitur*, "she would not be moved by the sense of maternal duty."

The most likely source of this *pietas* seems to be Euripides' *Alcestis*. Three times in the play we hear of Pheres' ἀψυχία (642-645; 696 f.; 717). It is for the lack of *pietas*, on the part of Pheres, that Admetus spells it out (641):

καί μ' οὐ νομίζω παῖδα σὸν πεφυκέναι.

That is to say, both his parents have lost the right to be called his true relatives (φίλοι):

338 στυγῶν μὲν ἥ μ' ἔτικτεν, ἐχθαίρων δ' ἐμὸν
    πατέρα· λόγῳ γὰρ ἦσαν, οὐκ ἔργῳ, φίλοι.
646 ...ἣν [sc. Alcestin] ἐγὼ καὶ μητέρα
    πατέρα τέ γ' ἐνδίκως ἂν ἡγοίμην μόνην.

As we learn from lines 75-78 (*Si vinco matrem, vinco pietate parentem...*)
and 102 f., Alcestis alone possesses this *pietas*. The source will be again
Euripides (*Alc.* 180-182). This line of interpretation finds support in the
way Plato treats Alcestis at *Symposion* 179 c 1, when stating that Alcestis
had surpassed Admetus' parents in the bond of love and family loyalty
(ὑπερεβάλετο τῇ φιλίᾳ). It is this simple *pietas* of Alcestis that wins over the
sophisticated philosophical erudition of Clymene.

(5) *Pheres as a Hedonist.* Pheres adduces two reasons for rejecting his
son's request to give his life for him. The main reason is: "There is
nothing sweeter to my heart than life alone" (39 f.: <*vi*>*ta quia dulcius
una / nil mihi*). This "hedonistic" argument may derive again from
Euripides' *Alcestis*, where Pheres expresses his *Lebensphilosophie* as follows:

691 χαίρεις ὁρῶν φῶς· πατέρα δ' οὐ χαίρειν δοκεῖς;
    ἦ μὴν πολύν γε τὸν κάτω λογίζομαι
    χρόνον, τὸ δὲ ζῆν μικρόν, ἀλλ' ὅμως γλυκύ.
722 φίλον τὸ φέγγος τοῦτο τοῦ θεοῦ, φίλον.

Pheres' second argument reads: "In order to enjoy the little life which
is left to my old age, I have already given my kingdom and my court to
you: what else do you want from me?" (38: *quam propter mea regna dedi tibi,
castra reliqui*). As Schäublin (176) pointed out, this argument too seems
to have been inspired by Euripides, where Pheres says:

686 ἃ δ' ἡμῶν χρῆν σε τυγχάνειν, ἔχεις.
    πολλῶν μὲν ἄρχεις, πολυπλέθρους δέ σοι γύας
    λείψω.

(6) *Clymene as a Stoic Philosopher.* The *Agon* between Clymene and
Alcestis, I would say, is the most original device of the Barcelona bard.
Clymene's elaborate philosophical reasoning (42-70) is here to counterbalance Alcestis' own *rhesis* (71-103), so that there can be little doubt that
the poet is introducing a *Certamen* between Mother and Wife here, in
which the latter's simple moral *pietas* prevails over the former's
philosophical sophistication.
    Clymene adduces no less than *five* different arguments to prove her
thesis that no member of a family should serve as a *stellvertretendes Opfer*
for another member, and particularly not a mother for her child. In her

anti-rhesis, Alcestis responds with three counter-arguments, for no *rhesis* may consist of a single argument.

Leaving Clymene's three less important arguments for the Commentary, her two main reasons come from *Stoic philosophy* (53-59 and 70-69). Apparently, Clymene enters the stage with Seneca in her right hand. For she opens her argument with an unmistakable Senecan echo (53): *Cur metui <s> mortem, cui nascimur?* ("Why are you afraid of death for which we all are born?"). Compare Seneca *Ad Marciam* 10.5.

Clymene keeps quoting Stoic philosophy (57 f.):

> Perpetuum nihil est, nihil est sine morte creatum:
> lux rapitur et nox oritur, moriuntur et anni.

Compare again Seneca *Ad Polybium* 1.1: *Ita est: nihil perpetuum, pauca diuturna sunt; aliud alio modo fragile est, rerum exitus variantur, ceterum quicquid coepit et desinit.* The idea of *moriuntur et anni* is basically Stoic too, but in Stoa the stress is on the *eternity* of the whole universe, not on the perishability of its parts (compare Seneca *Epist.* 24.26; Philo *De aeternitate mundi* 109).

Finally, Clymene closes her *perpetuum nihil est* argument with a forceful climax-*gradatio* (69), consisting of 2 + 3 + 4 + 5 syllables:

> 70   Nam qu<a>ecumque tegit <ca>eli v<i>s vel vagus aër
> 69   cedunt labuntur moriuntur contumulantur.

("For whatever lives under the heavenly ether and the roaming air passes away, perishes, dies, and is buried forever"). Lebek (25) has successfully healed line 70 by means of Ovid *Met.* 1.26-29. But the point is that the idea of the Earth being encompassed by the fiery ether (*ignea... vis caeli*) and by the light, roving air (*proximus est aër illi levitate locoque*) is Stoic again (compare, e.g., Franz Bömer ad Ovid *Met.* 1.26). What may be more important, however, the climax of 69 expresses the old Heraclitean and Stoic idea of πάντα ῥεῖ.

Clymene's second main argument is equally Stoic. It deals with the Stoic teaching of the inevitability of Fate. Our poet employs the image of the extreme East, West, North or South, beloved in Latin poetry, to convey the idea, "Escape to the *end* of the world!" (53 f.: *effuge longe, / quo..., quo..., ubi...*). Now, Clymene stresses her point of inevitability of personal fate (56):

> illic, nate, late: <ibi> te tua fata sequentur

("My son, go and hide there: and <there> your fate will reach you!") by employing alliteration, anaphora, and a *hiatus in caesura*—all in one single line. But the point is that the line echoes Seneca's famous dictum (*Epist.* 107.11.5): *Ducunt volentem fata, nolentem trahunt.*

At first glance, Clymene's argument about the inevitability of Fate sounds persuasive, especially when she forcefully states (64): *Cur ego de nato doleam, quem fata reposcunt?* ("Why should I grieve for a son who is claimed by his destiny?"). Her statement implies: "It would be a sacrilege for me to interfere with the decree of Fate: Ἀνάγκη οὐδὲ θεοὶ μάχονται." But her argument is shaky. For the reader already knows that the Fates are willing to make an *exception* with Admetus by accepting a substitute victim—*tu poteris posthac alieno vivere fato* (17). Either our poet was carried away by his rhetorical zeal, or he wanted to present Clymene as an utterly *nocens, inproba,* and *inproperans* person (45 f.).

(7) *Alcestis' pietas*. Alcestis' *anti-rhesis* falls into two parts. In its first part (71-82), she tries to demonstrate why she should sacrifice her life for her husband. In the second part (83-103), she entreats Admetus not to forget her after her death, and to take good care of her small orphans. Now, it is amazing to learn that in both parts our *poeta doctus* was able to borrow wisdom from Euripides' *Alcestis*, Propertius' Cornelia (4.11) and Cynthia (4.7), Silius Italicus (5.636-639), and most probably from Vergil's Dido, and Ovid's Laodamia (*Heroid.* 13.157 f.) as well. Since the heroine's religious philosophy (σωφροσύνη) plays the major part in this *ethopoeia*, we must take a closer look at her main arguments.

Alcestis' first main reason is that her self-denying death will secure an immense and everlasting glory for her: *laus magna mei post funera nostra* (76). For her noble feat will be remembered through centuries and generations to come (for example, in the present poem). The source of this argument may be seen again in Euripides' *Alcestis* 623 f.: πάσαις δ' ἔθηκεν εὐκλεέστερον βίον / γυναιξίν. This seems to be in accord with the traditional myth; compare *Alcesta* 154 [= *Aen.* 7.2 and 9.249]: *aeternam moriens famam tam certa tulisti*.

Alcestis' second main reason, on which her *laus magna* depends, is crucial for the understanding of the entire poem. As we have already seen (in point 4), it is her *pietas*, "the sense of duty of a family-member" (45; 75; 103). Unlike Pheres and Clymene, Alcestis alone possesses this sense of duty of a φίλος. It is her only but powerful weapon.

What was the source of inspiration for our poet in presenting Alcestis as an *exemplum pietatis* (103), one may ask? Maybe the heroine possessed an *inborn* sense of piety (εὐσέβεια)? For while the rest of Pelias' daughters (Pelopia, Medusa, Pisidice, and Hippothoe) enganged in the killing of their father, Alcestis, the oldest daughter, refused to take part in this crime: μόνην δ' Ἄλκηστιν δι' εὐσεβείας ὑπερβολὴν ἀποσχέσθαι τοῦ γεννήσαντος (says Diodorus 4.52.2). And it is as a reward for this piety that Alcestis was given to Admetus to be his wedded wife, continues Diodorus

(6.8.1: μόνην τῆς κατὰ τὸν πατέρα ἀσεβείας οὐ μετασχοῦσαν δοθῆναι γυναῖκα δι' εὐσέβειαν 'Αδμήτῳ). Consequently, the possibility that our learned poet, in depicting Alcestis as an ideal *coniux pia* (78), was employing the myth of the killing of Pelias I think cannot be ruled out.

Still, I prefer to search for the source of Alcestis' *pietas* in Euripides' *Alcestis* alone. For there she feels, not to give her life for her husband would be equal to a *betrayal* (προδοῦναι) of their marital bond and family commitment. While bidding farewell to her marriage bed—a sacred symbol of her bond with her husband (compare Sophocles *Trach*. 915-922; *Odyssey* 23.183-201),—Alcestis states (180-182):

180   προδοῦναι γάρ σ' ὀκνοῦσα καὶ πόσιν
         θνήσκω. σὲ δ' ἄλλη τις γυνὴ κεκτήσεται,
         σώφρων μὲν οὐκ ἂν μᾶλλον, εὐτυχὴς δ' ἴσως.

("I die because I hated to *betray* you and my husband. Now, another wife will obtain you. More fortunate than I? Perhaps. Wiser than I? Never."). In brief, Alcestis' σωφροσύνη, her "ethical and religious wisdom," finds its expression in her readiness to sacrifice her life for her husband, to fulfill her duty deriving from the bond, obligation and loyalty between the spouses (*pietas*). Or, as Alcestis herself put it (74): *pro coniuge coniux*.

(8) *Imagination and inventiveness.* In addition to his Alexandrian erudition, this seems to be the most striking characteristic of the Barcelona bard. His vivid, and sometimes even wild, imagination is reflected in every one of the five parts of the poem. For example, in part I Admetus surprises us with a strange theory (5-8), according to which a person's spirit or soul (*animus*) and his "self" (*ego*) have different destinies after the death: the soul (ψυχή) ascends to "the starry sphere," while the "self" (presumably, a person's shadow or εἴδωλον) goes either to the μακάρων νῆσοι or to the gloomy realm of Acheron.

In part II, Pheres comes up with a surprise offer of two eyes or one hand for his son (32-35). Where does the idea of such substitute body-parts come from, one may ask? Pheres' second offer (40-42) is equally puzzling: he may be willing to *lend* his remaining years to his son, provided that the latter is equally willing to *return* them to him in the future.

In part III, Clymene matches her husband's strange offer with another *adynaton* (51 f.): she may be willing to sacrifice her life for her son if only this could make him remain on earth *forever*.

The biggest surprise, however, awaits the reader in part IV of the poem. Unlike the Euripidean Alcestis (cf. vv. 305; 308; 372 f.), and unlike the *Alcesta* of *A.L.* (cf. vv. 125-128), our Alcestis does take into consideration the possibility of a second wife for Admetus (cf. vv. 83-85; 98; 102 f.). As we shall see in the Commentary, she does so either under the influence of Propertius' *regina elegiarum* (4.11.85-90), or due to an apparent inconsistency in Euripides (*Alc.* 181: σὲ δ' ἄλλη τις γυνὴ κεκτήσεται). All our Alcestis demands from her husband is for her to remain his *first and greatest love* (84 f.: *vestigia ne mea coniux / carior ista legat*). In other words, Admetus' second wife, naturally enough, would take Alcestis' place in his *household*, but not in his *heart* as well. It should be a marriage of necessity for a young widower with small children, not of love, implies our Alcestis. Now, I take the idea that Admetus' first wife should remain his *greatest* love (*on revient toujours à ses premières amours*) to be a fruit of the poet's vivid imagination.

This suggestion seems to find support in another innovation introduced by our poet. He was not satisfied with the *statue-motif* of Alcestis/Laodamia/Cornelia as found in Euripides (*Alc.* 348-352), Ovid (*Heroid.* 13.151-158), and Propertius (4.11.83 f.). According to Euripides, Admetus would order the best sculptors to make an effigy of his late wife, which he would embrace and caress, and even talk to it. Our poet exploits this motif in his lines 86-88. But he decided to combine the effigy-motif (86: *meque puta tecum sub nocte iacere*) with the strange idea of the shadow of Alcestis coming to *sleep with her living husband* during the night (90: *si redeunt umbr<a>e, veniam tecum<que> iacebo*). Most probably, he did so under the influence of Propertius' Cynthia (4.7.1-4 and 89). But my point is that this is the product of a wild imagination.

Finally, in part V the poet employs no less than three chthonic deities to deprive Alcestis of her daylight (117-124): *Hora fatalis* (117), *Mors* (123, resembling the Euripidean *Thanatos*), and an *Infernus deus* (124), most probably *Dis pater* or *Pluto*. This is another exaggeration which one may expect from a young poet.

(9) *Poeta doctus.* The Barcelona poet displays a rich repertoire of precious folkloric and mythological motifs. In addition to what has been already mentioned, compare the following motifs. "The tantamount life-span" (transfer of the years of life allotted to one person to the account of another person) in lines 17 (*alieno vivere fato*), 29 (*si tempora dones*), 73 f. (*ego tempora dono, / Admete, <e>ventura tibi*).[5] *Obiectus pectorum*, on the part of Clymene (48: *haec ubera*), and a mother's *womb and breasts* as a sacred principle of life, and as such a *taboo* (48-50).[6] The world-era (*Magnus*

---

[5] Cf. *Hypothesis* to Eurip. *Alc.*; Propert. 4.11.95; Ovid. *Met.* 7.168; Tibull. 1.6.63 f.; *C.L.E.* 995.13-16 and 25 f.; Stith Thompson, *Motif-Index of Folk Literature* E165; D1855.2; T211.1.

[6] Cf. Stat. *Theb.* 11.341 f.; Porphyry *Vita Pyth.* 45, ἀπέχεσθαι... μήτρας.

annus) of the miraculous bird Phoenix (54 f.: *iteratus... orbis*).[7] The catalogue of the "dying gods" in 60-63: the tomb of Zeus in Crete; the
catabasis of Demeter in search of Persephone; the myth of the small boy
Dionysus being lured by the tricky Titans and then dismembered;
finally, the descent to hell of Aphrodite to bring back Adonis. The latter
two motifs are less frequent. For the myth of the *Bacchus dissectus* compare
Aristides *Apol.* 10.8 (and Geffcken, p. 70); Justin 1 *Apol.* 21.2; Clement
Protr. 17.2; Arnob. *Adv. nat.* 1.41; 5.19; (Origen *c. Cels.* 3.23; *Acta
Apollonii* 22); while the myth of the *catabasis* of Aphrodite is known from
Aristides alone (*Apol.* 11.3).[8]

Showing off his mythological erudition, the Barcelona bard combines
the catalogue of the "dying gods" with the catalogue of the heroines losing their sons (65-68): Diomede lost her son Hyacinthus; Agave even tore
her son Pentheus asunder. Althaea killed Meleager, and so did the goddess Ino with her son Melicertes. On top of that, Procne bewailed her
son Itys, she herself had dismembered, while collecting his bleeding
entrails. Here again our poet proves his erudition: the name of Hyacinthus' mother (Diomede) is a mythological rarity.

Furthermore, the motif of a mother continuing to live after her death
in her orphans, provided that they resemble their mother (96 f.), and the
popular motif of the faithful dead mother *avenging* her maltreated orphans
even from her grave (98 f.: *ne... flentes matris pia vindicet umbra*).[9] The motif
of the pious heroine *personally* preparing her own funeral pyre (110-116).
Last but not least, the motif of the cold *hand of Death* (117 f.).[10]

It may be worth mentioning that Pliny in particular was a preferred
source of information for our poet in looking for exotic erudition. For
example, the world-era of Phoenix in 54 f. (*N.H.* 10.5 and 29.29); the
seismic activity of Earth, devouring the very places she herself had
previously produced, alluded to in line 59 (*N.H.* 2.205, as Lebek had
correctly pointed out); the belief that amomum comes from a bird's nest
(especially the bird Phoenix), in line 114 (*N.H.* 12.85, as the Oxonienses
had convincingly pointed out); finally, the *pallida balsama* of line 113
(*N.H.* 12.48 and 13.17: *pallidum amomum*), and the pulverized amomum
of line 114 (*N.H.* 12.49: *friatum amomum*).

---

[7] Cf. Pliny *N.H.* 10.5 and 29.29; Claudian *Carm. min.* 27.104 f. et alibi. See R. van
den Broek, *The Myth of the Phoenix*, Leiden, 1971, 67-112.

[8] Cf., e.g., Cicero *N.D.* 1.42; 1.119; 3.53 [and A.S. Pease ad loc.]; Callim. *In Iovem*
8 f.; Tatian *Orat.* 27; Athenag. *Legat.* 30; Clem. *Protr.* 37.4; Arnob. *Adv. nat.* 4.25, as for
the *Iuppiter Cretensis*; Hygin. *Fab.* 251; Orphic Hymn 41.5; Clem. *Protr.* 17.1; Vergil
Georg. 1.39; Schol. Pindar *Ol.* 6.160a; Suda, s.v. βάραθρον, as for the catabasis of
Demeter; G. Harrison, D. Obbink, *ZPE* 63 (1986) 75-81, esp. 76 f.

[9] Cf. Stith Thompson, E221.2.1; E323.2, et alibi.

[10] Cf. Verg. *Aen.* 10.419; *C.L.E.* 995.8, et alibi.

(10) *Poetic diction*. As both the apparatus to the Translation and the Commentary show, Lucretius, Vergil, Horace, Propertius, Ovid, Tibullus, Seneca, Lucan, Silius, and Statius were the major sources of poetic inspiration for our poet. Two important sources should be added to this list. First, the poet was a very attentive reader of Euripides' *Alcestis*. And second, he stands under an undeniable spell of the popular Latin sepulchral poetry, such as is represented by *Carmina Latina Epigraphica*.

Apparently, the main stylistic device employed by the poet to express the *ethos* and the *pathos* of his heroine is a frequent usage of *anaphora*, which is to be found in these lines: 3 (*da*); 5 (*quae...*, *quid*); 10 f. (/ *suc-cepi...*, / *accepi*); 18 (*cum*); 27 f. (*hoc... docuere...*, *hoc... / ... edocuit*); 29 (*tu*); 29 f. (*si*); 32 (*genitor*); 47 f. (*tu*); 50 f. (*hostis*); 54 (*quo*); 56 (*illic...: <ibi>*); 57 (*nihil*); 64 f. (/ *cur ego*); 65 (*plangam... planxere*); 67 (*perdidit*); 72 (*me... trade*); 75 f. (*si* and *vinco*); 81 f. (*me*); 83 f. (*ne*); 86 (*me*); 93 f. (*pignora*); 100 (*si*); 103 (*disce* = Silius 5.637 f.); 123 (*venit*).

Alliterations abound, and are present in no less than 71 out of a total of 122 extant lines.[11] *Versus Leonini* occur in lines 6; 55; 95; 115 and 116. The effect of the *hiatus in caesura* is present in lines 22; 35; 50 (?) and 56 (?).

Furthermore, take notice of the *thematic* polyptoton, *pro coniuge coniux* / (74); of the force and expression of such moral injunctions of the pious Alcestis as these: *coniux, ne desera<r> a te, / ... quod vitam desero pro te* / (91 f.); *Et tu pro coniuge cara / disce mori!* (102 f.); or of the proverbial antithesis, *maestusque beato / iactat membra toro* (21 f.), attesting to the old truth that no wealth of this world can buy happiness.

Last but not least, compare the rhyme-chain in lines 60-63 (*abisse / ... obisse / ... perisse / ... subisse* /), which is employed to stress Clymene's point, "even the gods die—one after the other!" Or the paronomasia, *me portet... Porthmeus!* (82), "let me be carried away by the Carrier!" (cf. *C.L.E.* 1223.7: *portabit Portitor*). Or else the pointed climax in Clymene's closing line (69), *cedunt labuntur moriuntur contumulantur* (2 + 3 + 4 + 5 syllables).

The other side of the coin is represented by the shortcomings of late Latin poetry. One of them consists in a dull repetition of the same word.

---

[11] *Alliterations*: 1-2 (*p* and *l*); 4-5 (*f*); 6 (*a*); 10 (*d*); 12 (*p*); 13 (*m* and *a*); 16 (*i* and *c*); 17 (*p*); 18 (*g*); 18-19 (*c*); 20 (*t*); 30 (*m* and *sub-*); 33 (*c*); 34 (*m*); 35 (*s*); 37 (*v* and *m*); 38 (*r*); 39 (*t*); 40 (*m*); 41 (*ss*); 43 (*v*); 44-45 (*f*); 45 (*n*); 47 (*m*); 48 (*t*); 51 (*v*); 52 (*s* and *r*); 53 (*m*); 54 (*a*); 55 (*n*); 55-56 (*i* and *t*); 57 (*n/m*); 65 (*p*); 66-67 (*a*); 68 (*i* and *c*); 70 (*v*); 69 (*u*); 75 (*p*); 76 (*m/n*); 78-79 (*a* and *t*); 82 (*m* and *p*); 83-84 (*m/n*); 85 (*n*); 88-89 (*t*); 91-92 (*d*); 93-94 (*p*); 96-97 (*m* and *r*); 98-99 (*p*); 102 (*c*); 103 (*m*); 105 (*r* and *a*); 107 (*v*); 110 (*p*); 113-115 (*p*); 116 (*o*); 117 (*p*); 118 (*r*); 120 (*f*); 121 (*i* and *f*); 124 (*m*?).

Such as *edocet... docuere... edocuit* (25, 27, 28); *concedere... concedam... concessissem... concedere... concedo* (31, 33, 41, 51, 73); *tumuloque... tumulosque... tumulosque... tumulis... tumulatus... contumulantur* (20, 30, 41, 48, 60, 69); *me trade sepulcris* (72, 81); *moritura... moritura... peritura... moritura* (83, 97, 107, 119).

Another characteristic, witnessing to a lack of poetic originality, may be called "centonic procedure." For example, the ease with which our poet was able to put Flaminius' words (Silius 5.636-639) into the mouth of Alcestis (103) is disturbing. So is the way in which the Ovidian expression, *pro coniuge coniux*, could become a *principle* for Alcestis (74). Line 93 is a centonic borrowing from Propertius (4.11.73), and such borrowed clausulae as (100) *dulcis imago* /, or (121) *fugientis imago* / simply fail to convince. All this may speak in favor of the assumption that the Barcelona bard was a young late Latin poet of a modest talent, but with great poetic ambitions.

TEXT AND TRANSLATION

P 158a　　"Pr<a>escie Lauripotens, Latonie Deli<e> P<a>ean:
　　　　invoco te laurusque tuo de nomine lectas.
　　　　<Arcitenens,> da scire diem, da noscere, quando
　　　　rumpant Admeti fatalia fila Sorores.
5　　　Quae finis vitae, qui<d> mi post fata relinquant,
　　　　edoce, siderea<s> animus quando ivit in auras.
　　　　Quamvis scire homini, ni prospera vita futura <est>,
　　　　tormentum (sit<ne> atra dies et pallida regna?),
　　　　ede tamen, si te colui famulumque paventem
10　　succepi pecudumque ducem post crimina divum
　　　　accepi iussi<que> idem dare iubila silvis."

1 presciae *et* latoniaeae *P* | lauripotens : apollo *superscripsit P* | Deli<e> P<a>ean
*Lebek, Parsons (cf. v.*12) : dolipiant *P* || 2 -que tuo *Lebek, Parsons, Marcovich* : quemtuus
P | nomine *P* : numine *Parsons* | lectas *Marcovich (cf. v.*70 tegit : legit *P*; *v.*85 legat : tegat
P) : [[t]]ςectas *P* (*ut videtur*) : certas *Parsons* : certam (*sc. v.*3 diem) *Shackleton Bailey* || 3
<Arcitenens> *e.g. suppl. Marcovich* : apollo *contra metrum P* (*cf. v.*1 lauripotens : apollo
ss. P) || 5 qui<d> *Ed.* : qui *P* | mi *Hutchinson, Nisbet* : me *P* | relinqua[[nt]]m *P* ||
6 aedoce *P* : me doce *coni. Lebek, J. K. Newman* | siderea<s> *Lebek, Parsons, Marcovich*
: siderea *P* | animus *Ed.*: animum *P* | ivit *Marcovich* (*coll. Dracont. Orest.* 447) : ibit *Führer,
Watt, Tandoi, Koenen* (*coll. Ovid. Her.* 10.121; *Tr.* 1.5.11 *sq.*) : luit *P* : exit *Parsons* || 7
quamuis scire *P* : quae nescire *Hutchinson* | hominis *P* | ni *Marcovich* : sit *P, retinet Lebek*
: seu *Hutchinson, Nisbet* | futura <est> *Nisbet* : futuri *P* : futura *Lebek* || 8 sit<ne> *Mar-
covich, Tandoi* : sit *P* : sit, <an> *Lebek* : sive *Hutchinson, Nisbet* | regna *Marcovich, Watt*
(*cf. v.*7 uita *P et v.*13 *sq.* Acherontis... regna; *v.*61 fratri<s> Stygii regnum) : uitam *P*
: vita *Ed., agn. Lebek, Parsons* : fata *Nisbet* || 9 aede *P* | sinonte *P, corr. Lebek, Parsons,
Marcovich* | famolumquee *P* || 10 pe[[q]] `c´udumque *P* | crimine *P* || 11 iossi *P* |
-<que> *add. Lebek, Parsons, Marcovich* | *post* siluis *addit P* : ʃ apollo (*i.e., notam personae
loquentis*) *in mg. dextra* ||

"O, Delian Paean, son of Latona! O prescient Lord of laurels! I invoke you along with the laurels select because of your name. <O, Bow-bearer, > grant me to know the day of my death; grant me to learn when the Fates will break the life-thread of Admetus! Tell me, what will be the end of my life, and what Destiny may have in store for me once my spirit has gone into the starry sphere! I know, unless a man's life after death <is> a blessed one, it is anguish for him to know this (is it going to be a life without light, a realm of shadows?). Nevertheless, tell me, if I worshiped you ever; if I ever gave you shelter when you came to me as a terrified servant after the gods' charge against you; if I ever accepted you to be my herdsman, and I myself sent you to the forests to raise shouts of joy!"

Lauripotens : *solus Martianus Capella* 1.24 | Latonie : *Hostius ap. Macrob. Sat.* 6.5.8 (| arquitenens Latonius) || **4** fila Sorores | : *Lucan.* 6.703; *Silius* 3.96; 17.361; *Statius Silvae* 1.4.123; *C.L.E.* 443.4 *sq.*; 456.4; 1011.5; 1114.4 || **5** fata relinquant | : *Ovid. Met.* 14.153 || **6** ivit in auras | : *Ovid. Heroid.* 10.121; *Trist.* 1.5.11 *sq.* || **7** prospera vita : *Lucan.* 8.625; 8.631 *sq.* || **8** atra dies : *Verg. Aen.* 6.429; 11.28; *C.L.E.* 1036.2; 1262.4; 1385.12; 1401.2 *et saepius* | pallida regna | : *Silius* 11.472; 13.408; *Verg. Aen.* 8.244 *sq.*; *Lucan.* 1.456 || **9** si te colui : *Eurip. Alc.* 10 *sq.*; *Statius Theb.* 6.374 *et* 377 || **10** post crimina divum : *Eurip. Alc.* 6 *sq.*; *Stat. Theb.* 6.375-78; *Lucian. De sacrif.* 4 *et alibi* || **11** iussi-<que> idem : *Hygin. Fab.* 51.2; *Stat. Theb.* 6.377 *sq.* ||

Pr < a > escius < h > eu P < a > ean: "Doleo, sed vera fatebo < r > :
mors vicina premit m < a > estique Ac < h > eron < t > is adire
iam prope regna tibi gratamque relinquere lucem.

15 Sed veniat, pro te qui mortis damna subire
possit et instantis in se convertere casus,
tu poteris posthac alieno vivere fato.
Iam tibi cum genitor, genetrix cum car < a > supersit
et coniux natique rudes, pete, lumina pro te

20 qui claudat fatoque tuo tumuloque cremetur."

---

12 prescius *P* | < h > eu *coni. Lebek* : eu *P* : en *Parsons* : hic *Lebek, Hutchinson (coll. v.*32)
: et *vel* at *Watt* | P < a > ean *Lebek, Parsons (cf. v.*1) : pian *P* | seo *et* fatebo *P, corr. Ed.*
|| **13** *post* mors *addit* inquid *P, del. Ed.* | uicinam *P* | m < a > estique *Hutchinson, Marcovich*
: mestumque *P* | aceronis *P, corr. Ed. (p.* 49) || **15** subiret *P* || **16** possit *P* : poscat *olim*
*Marcovich (coll. v.*32) | casum *P* || **17** posthac *Ed.*: [[.]]posthacṣ *P (ut videtur)* || **18** qum...
qum *P* | genitor *Lebek, Parsons, Marcovich* : genitụm *P* | car *et* susupersit *P* || **19** -que *Ed.*
: quae *P* || **20** qui *Ed.* : quae *P* ||

(12) Alas! Such was the answer of the prescient Paean: "I grieve for you, but I must tell the truth. Close death is pressing upon you: the time has come for you to abandon the dear light of day and approach the gloomy realm of Acheron. And yet, should somebody come forward having the heart to suffer death for you, to take on himself your impending misfortune, you will be granted henceforth to live the destiny of somebody else. Why, your father, your dear mother are still alive; and so are your wife and your young children. Go and ask them who may be willing to shut his eyes forever for you, to be burnt on the pyre as a substitute for your fate and grave."

12 vera fatebo<r> | : *Stat. Achill.* 1.146; *Ovid. Heroid.* 8.97; 14.47; *Pont.* 3.1.79; 3.9.19 || **13** mors vicina : *Lucan.* 7.50; *Seneca Epist.* 30.7 | m<a>estique Ac<h>eron<t>is... regna : *Silius* 14.243; *Culex* 273 || **15** mortis damna : *Ulpian. Dig.* 13.6.5.7 || **17** alieno vivere fato | : *Ovid. Met.* 15.90; *cf. vv.*29 *et* 73 *sq.*; *Euripid. Alcestis Hypoth.*; *Propert.* 4.11.95; *Ovid. Met.* 7.168; *Tibull.* 1.6.63 *sq.*; *C.L.E.* 995.13-16 *et* 25 *sq.* || **19** et coniux natique rudes : *Lucan.* 4.396 ||

ILLE LAREM POST DICTA PETIT M < A > ESTUSQUE BEATO
IACTAT MEMBRA TORO ET FLETIBUS ATRIA CONPLET.
AD NATUM GENITOR TRISTE < M > CONCURRIT ET ALTO
PECTORE SUSPIRANS LACRIMIS < QUAE > CAUSA REQUIRIT.
25 EDOCET ILLE PATREM FATORUM DAMNA SUORUM:
"ME RAPIT, ECCE, DIES, GENITOR: PARA FUNERA NATO.
HOC PARC < A > E DOCUERE NEFAS, HOC NOSTER APOLLO |

P 158b INVITUS, PATER, EDOCUIT. SE < D > REDDERE VITAM
TU, GENITOR, TU, SANCTE, POTES: SI TEMPORA DONES,
30 SI PRO ME MORTEM SUBITAM TUMULOSQUE SUBIRE
DIGNE < R > IS NATOQUE TUA < M > CONCEDERE LUCEM."

---

21 m < a > estusque *Parsons, Marcovich* : mestumque *P* : m < a > estumque (*adv.*) *Lebek* ||
22 toro et *P* : *hiatum in caesura in vv.* 35, 50, 56 *habes* || **23** triste < m > *Parsons, Marcovich*
: triste *P* : *retinet* (*ut adv.*) *Lebek* || **24** lacrimis < quae > *Nisbet* (*unius vocis lacunam in vv.*
7, 11, 49, 54, 56, 63, 72, 90, 107, 122, 124 *habes*) : lacrimarum *P*, *retinet Lebek* | causa
P : causa < m > *Lebek* | requeret *P* || **25** suorum *Lebek* : sororum *P* (*cf. v.* 4), *retinent Oxo-*
nienses || **26** dies *Lebek, Parsons* : uides *P* | genitur *P* (*ut videtur; cf. v.* 29) | para (∪ ∪) :
cf. v. 6 edoce (– ∪ ∪) || **27** *ante* hoc *addit P* : pa *in mg. sinistra* [*i.e., sive* Pa(rcae) *sive* pa(ter)]
| Parc < a > e docuere nefas *Lebek, Parsons* : parcedoquerenufas *P* | docuere : cecinere
Hutchinson : dixere *Nisbet* : nevere *Watt, Shackleton Bailey* : volvere *Tandoi* || **28** se < d >
Lebek, Parsons : se *P* || **29** admet(us) *addit P in mg. sinistra* | genitur *P* (*cf. v.* 26) || **30**
tumulosque *Lebek, Hutchinson, Nisbet, Marcovich* : tumulisque *P* || **31** digne < r > is nato-
que *Ed.* : digneosnatosque *P* | tua < m > *Lebek* : tuo *P* ||

(21) Having learnt this, Admetus returns to his home. Stricken with grief he cannot help tossing his limbs on the rich couch, while his weeping reaches every corner of the palace. The father hurries to his sorrowful son, and sighing from the depth of his breast asks him the reason for these tears. The son tells his father about his premature death: "Father, my day of death is carrying me away: prepare a funeral for your son! This awful mishap was revealed by the Fates, it was revealed—reluctantly— by our Apollo. And yet, you, father, you, the venerable one, can restore my life—if you only would donate the rest of your days to me; if you would deign to grant your own life to your son, to suffer sudden death and approach the grave for me!''

---

22 iactat membra toro : *Iuvenalis* 13.218; *Verg. Aen.* 6.220 *et alibi* | atria conplet | : *Ovid. Met.* 5.153 || **23-24** alto | pectore suspirans : *Verg. Aen.* 6.599 *sq.*; 2.288 [= *Alcesta* 92]; *Silius* 9.151 *sq.*; *Ovid. Met.* 1.656 *sq.*; 2.655 *sq.* | lacrimis ... causa : *Verg. Aen.* 3.305; *Lucan.* 3.607 || **25** fatorum damna suorum | : *Ovid. Trist.* 1.8.47 *sq.*; *Silius* 4.708; *C.L.E.* 965.3 || **26** funera nato | : *Ovid. Ibis* 583; *Stat. Theb.* 9.365 || **27** nefas : *C.L.E.* 1225.2 *sq.* | noster Apollo | : *Stat. Theb.* 3.627 *sq.* || **28** reddere vitam | : *Ovid. Ibis* 405; *C.L.E.* 386.6 || **29** | tu, genitor : *Verg. Aen.* 2.717 | si tempora dones : *Lucan.* 9.534 || **30** mortem subitam : *Verg. Aen.* 11.796; *Martialis* 6.53.3 *et saepius* || **31** concedere lucem : *Claudian.* 28.128 *sq.* ||

HIC GENITOR, NON UT GENITOR: "SI LUMINA POSCAS,
CONCEDAM, GRATEQUE MANUM DE CORPORE NOSTRO,
NATE, VELIS, TRIBUAM: VIVET MANUS ALTERA MECUM;
35   SI SINE LUMINE <E>RO, ALIQUID TAMEN ESSE VIDEBOR:
NIL ERO, SI QU<O>D SUM DONAVERO. QUANTA SENECT<A>E
VITA MEAE SUPEREST, MINIMAM VI TOLLERE V<I>S IAM?
QUAM PROPTER MEA REGNA DEDI TIBI, CASTRA RELIQUI.
CONT<R>ISTANT TUMUL<I>, <VI>TA QUIA DULCIUS UNA
40   NIL MIHI. POST MORTEM QUAM TU SI REDDERE VELLES,
NATE, TIBI CONCESSISSEM TUMULOSQUE <H>ABITASSE<M>,
VISURUS POST FATA DIEM."   PULSUS GENETRICIS

---

32 *post* genitor *addit* gens *P, del. Lebek, Parsons* | *post* poscas *addit P* : ʃ ʃ pa(ter) *in mg. dextra*
|| **33** grateque *Hutchinson* : gratamque *P, retinet Lebek* || **34** uellis *P* || **35** lumine | ro
P, corr. Ed. || **36** nihil *P, corr. Ed. (cf. v.*40) | si qu<o>d sum *Ed.* : sicutsuum *P* | senecte
P || **37** vita meae *Ed.* : uitaemeae *P* : extremae *Nisbet* | vi *Marcovich* : uis *P* | v<i>s
iam? *Marcovich* : ustam *vel fortasse* u[[s]]itam *P* : vitam? *Parsons* : v<i>s tu *Lebek* || **38**
quam *Ed.* : quem *P* : quapropter? *Tandoi* | mea *Hutchinson* : quea *P* : quia *Lebek, Parsons*
| regna *Lebek, Parsons* : regnam *P* : regnum *Ed.* | deds *P* | relinqui *P* || **39** cont<r>istant
tumul<i> *Lebek et* <vi>ta quia *Marcovich (cf. v.*37 uitae *P)* : contustanttomultaequam
P : contentus tantum vita, qua *Shackleton Bailey* | dulcius una *Hutchinson* : dulciorullam
P || **40** nihil *P, corr. Ed. (cf. v.*36) | si *Ed.* : fi *P* : sic *Parsons* | velles *Ed.* : uellis *P* : posses
Hutchinson || **41** tibi *Hutchinson (cf. v.*50 meae *P)* : tuo *P* : tua *(sc. vita) Shackleton Bailey*
| concessissem *Lebek (ob caesuram cf. vv.* 28, 32, 48, 74, 78, 80, 88, 96) : concessissesem
P : cessisse velim *Hutchinson, Nisbet* | tumulosque *Ed., Lebek* : edtumulusque *P* |
<h>abitasse<m> *Lebek, Marcovich* : abitasse *P* || **42** di[[u]]ʃe´m *P* | pulsusque *P, corr.*
Ed. ||

(32) Hear now the father speaking unlike a father: "Should you ask me for my eyes, I would grant them to you. Should you want a hand from my body, my son, I would gladly give it to you. Still I would be left with the other hand, and though deprived of sight, I would still have the appearance of a living being. But if I grant you my very being, there will be nothing left of me. Little life is left to my old age: are you after even this little to snatch it away before its time? Why, it was to enjoy this brief life of mine that I have given my kingdom to you, that I have left my court to you. Of the grave I dare not think: there is nothing sweeter to my heart than life alone. My son, I would gladly give my life for you and go to the grave, if only you were equally willing to return it some day to me, enabling me to see the daylight again!"

32 si lumina poscas | : *Ovid. Fasti* 2.351 *sq.* || **33** manum de corpore nostro | : *Iuvenalis* 13.92; *Ovid. Heroid.* 19.84 || **37** minimam : *Eurip. Alc.* 649 *sq.* || **38** | quam propter : *Verg. Aen.* 12.177 | mea regna : *Verg. Aen.* 2.543; *Ecl.* 1.69 | castra reliqui | : *Verg. Aen.* 10.604; *Lucan.* 2.563; *Ovid. Met.* 13.522; *Eurip. Alc.* 686-88 || **39-40** <vi>ta quia dulcius una | nil mihi : *Eurip. Alc.* 691-93; 715; 722 || **41** tumulosque <h>abitasse<m> : *Petron.* 71.7; *C.L.E.* 1267.3 *et saepius* ||

VOLVITUR ANTE PEDES, VESTIGIA BLANDUS ADORAT
44   INQUE SINUS FUNDIT LACRIMAS. FUGIT ILLA ROGANTEM,
P 159a   NEC PIETATE, NOCENS, | NEC VINCITUR INPROBA FLETU,
HAEC SUPER INPROPERANS: "OBLITUS MENTE PARENTUM
TU, SCELERATE, POTES MATERNA < M > CERNERE MORTE < M >,
TU TUMULIS GAUDERE MEIS? HAEC UBERA FLAMMAE
DIRIPIA < N > T, UTERUM < QUE > ROGI VIS ULTIMUS IGNIS
50   CONSUMAT, QUO TE PEPERI? HOSTIS MIHI LUCIS,
HOSTIS, NATE, PATRIS. VITAM CONCEDERE VELLEM,
SI SEMPER POSSES TER < R > ENA < IN > SEDE MORARI.

43 dante *P* | blandus *Lebek, Hutchinson, Nisbet, Marcovich* : ˋuˊ d ˋuˊ landus [*i.e., sive* blandus *sive* adulandus] *P* || **44** lacrimas *Lebek, Hutchinson, Marcovich* : lacrimum *P* : lacrimam *Ed.*, *Parsons* || **45** pietatem *P* | fletus *P* || **46** oblitus *P* : oblita *Hutchinson* || **47** *ante* tu *notam personae loquentis* mater *addit P in mg. sinistra* | materna < m > cernere morte < m > *Lebek, Parsons, Marcovich* : materna cernere morte *P* : materna vivere morte *Nisbet* || **48** ubira *P* || **49** diripia < n > t *Lebek, Hutchinson* : deripiat *P* : deripia < n > t *Ed.* | -< que > *add. Lebek, Parsons* | rogi *Parsons* : cogis *P* : rogis *Lebek* || **50** consumad *P* | quo te peperi *olim Lebek, Newman* : quodtepeperi *P* : qui te peperi < t > *Parsons* : quod te peperi < t > *Lebek et olim Marcovich* | mihi lucis *Marcovich* (*cf. v.*41) : meaelucis *P* : genetricis *Lebek, Nisbet* || **51** natae *P* || **52** semper *P* : superum *Hutchinson* | posses *Lebek, Hutchinson* : possis *P* | ter< r >ena *Marcovich* : aeternam *P* : aeterna *Ed.* : aeternum *Hutchinson* : terrarum *Nisbet* | < in > *add. Schackleton Bailey* | murari *P* ||

(42) Rejected by his father, Admetus throws himself before the feet of his mother, embraces them in reverence and adulation, and sheds tears in her lap. But she, in her wickedness, shuns the suppliant. She, the heartless one, would be won neither by his imploring nor by the sense of maternal duty. Worse still, she starts casting reproaches: "Are you out of your mind, you a criminal wretch? How can you forget your duty toward your parents? How can you watch the death of your own mother and enjoy seeing her grave? Is that what you want—that the flames of the pyre devour these breasts, that the final funeral pile takes away the very womb by which I gave you birth? You, son, a foe to my daylight, a foe to your own father! Still, I would gladly give my life for you, if only I were sure that you could remain on earth forever."

---

43 volvitur ante pedes : *Propert.* 3.8.12 | vestigia... adorat | : *Stat. Theb.* 12.817 || **44** inque sinus fundit lacrimas : *Ovid. Fasti* 4.522; *Heroid.* 6.70 || **45** | nec pietate... nec: *Verg. Aen.* 1.545 | nec vincitur... fletu : *Verg. Aen.* 4.438 *sq.* [= *Alcesta* 76 *sq.*] || **48-49** haec ubera ... | ... uterum<que> : *Stat. Theb.* 11.341 *sq.*; *Seneca Herc. Oet.* 925 *sq.*; *Stat. Theb.* 10.694 *sq.* || **49** ultimus ignis : *Seneca Herc. Oet.* 1609 *sq.* || **51** vitam concedere vellem | : *Verg. Aen.* 11.111 || **52** <in> sede morari | : *Ovid. Met.* 2.846; *Ars Amat.* 3.436; *Fl. Merobaudes De Christo* 6 ||

Cur metui<s> mortem, cui nascimur? Effuge longe,
quo Part<h>us, quo Medus Arabs<que>, ubi barbarus ales
55 nascitur, ac nobis iteratus fingitur orbis;
illic, nate, late: <ibi> te tua fata sequentur.
Perpetuum nihil est, nihil est sine morte creatum:
lux rapitur et nox oritur, moriuntur et anni.
Non<ne> est terra locos, quos egeneraverat ante?

53 sur *P* | metui<s> *Lebek, Parsons* : metui *P* | quicui *P* | effugaelongae *P* || **54**
Part<h>us, quo *Parsons* : partusque *P* : partus{que} *Ed., Lebek* | Medus Arabs<que>
Ed. : medusarabs *P* : Medus<que et> Arabs *Lebek* : mollis Arabs *Nisbet* || **55** nascitur,
ac nobis iteratus fingitur orbis *Marcovich* (*coll. testimoniis*) : nascitur adque nobis iteratum
[[.]]ṣingitur urbis *P* : ... fingitur orbus *Ed.* : nascitur adque novos iteratum ḟingitur ortus
Lebek : nascitur atque novis iteratus †cingitur urbis† *Parsons* : stinguitur atque novis
iteratus nascitur orsis *Hutchinson, Nisbet* : nascitur atque annis iteratus cingitur orbis
Koenen || **56** late: <ibi> te *Marcovich* (*hiatum in caesura in vv.* 22, 35, 50 *habes*) : latete
P : late, <sed> te *Hutchinson* : late, <at> te *Parsons* || **59** non (non<ne> *Marcovich*)
ēst terra locos, quos egeneraverat ante? *Lebek* (*coll. Plin. N.H.* 2.205) : non est terra locus
quo se genera[[b]] ʾuˊerat ante *P* : non est terra loco (*Parsons*) quo se generaverat
(secreverat *Nisbet*) ante *Oxonienses* : non est terra loco [i.q. statu, condicione], quo <r>es
generaverat ante *olim Marcovich* ||

(53) "Why are you afraid of death for which we all are born? Escape to the end of the world—there where the Parthian or Mede of Arab lives; there where the exotic bird (Phoenix) is born, so that mankind may imagine the birth of a new world-era. My son, go and hide there: and <there> your fate will reach you! Nothing lasts forever, nothing is born free from death. Daylight wanes, night takes its place, and the seasons die. Why, does not the Earth devour the very places she herself had previously produced?"

53 *Seneca Ad Marciam (Dial.*6).10.5; *Epist.* 24.20; *Eurip. Alc.* 418 *sq. et* 782 || **53-54** *Catull.* 11.2-12; *Horat. Carm.* 1.22.5-8; 2.6.1-4; *Lucan.* 1.15-18 *et alibi* || **54** barbarus ales | : *Ovid. Met.* 15.392 *sq.* || **55** *Plin. N.H.* 10.5 *et* 29.29; *Claudiani Carm. min.* 27 (*Phoenix*).104 *sq.*; *Herodot.* 2.73; *Seneca Epist.* 42.1; *Tacit. Annal.* 6.28; *Lactant. De ave Phoenice* 59-64 *et alibi* || **56** fata sequentur | : *Silius* 8.38; *Propert.* 2.22.19 || **57** *Seneca Ad Polybium (Dial.* 11). 1.1.; *Statius Silvae* 2.1.218 *sq.*; *Manil.* 1.515-517; *Horat. Carm.* 4.7.7 *sq.* || **58** lux rapitur : *Horatii l.l.* | moriuntur et anni : *Seneca Epist.* 24.26 || **59** *Plin. N.H.* 2.205; *Stat. Silvae* 2.1.209-211 *et* 218; *Theb.* 7.809-817 ||

60   Ipse pater mundi fertur tumulatus abisse
        et fratri <s> Stygii regnum mutatus obisse;
        Bacc<h>um fama refert <T>ita<nu>m ex arte perisse,
        per<que> vadum lethi Cererem Veneremque subisse.
64   Cur ego de nato doleam, quem fata reposcunt? |

P 159b   Cur ego non plangam, sicut planxere priores?
        Amisit natum Diomede, carpsit Agaue;
        perdidit Alt<ha>ea <g>natum, dea perdidit Ino;
68   flevit Ityn Progne, dum colligit ilia cruda.
70   Nam qu<a>ecumque tegit <ca>eli v<i>s vel vagus aër
69   cedunt labuntur moriuntur contumulantur.''

---

60 *ante* ipse *addit* P poe(ta) *in mg. sinistra* || **61** fratre P, *corr. Ed.* | Stygii *Hutchinson, Nisbet* (*cf. Verg. Aen.* 9.104 *et* 10.113) : stygium P, *retinet Lebek* | mutatus *Hutchinson, Marcovich* : multatus P, *retinet Lebek* || **62** baccum P | <T>ita<nu>m ex arte *Marcovich* (*cf. vv.*95 *et* 103) : itamdearte P : Titanum marte *Parsons* : <T>itanide <ab> arte *Lebek* || **63** per<que> vadum *Lebek, Parsons* : peruadam P : per vada *Ed.* | lethi *Lebek* : lechi P : leti *Parsons* : Lethe<s> *Hutchinson* || **64** reposcunt *Lebek, Nisbet* : deposcunt P || **66** admisit P | Diomede *Parsons* [*scil. mater Hyacinthi, Hutchinson*] : diomedes P | Agaue *Lebek, Parsons* : acatem P || **67** perdedit... perdedit P | Alt<ha>ea *Ed.* : alpea P : Althaee *Hutchinson* | <g>natum *Marcovich* : natum P | Ino *Lebek, Nisbet* : ion P || **68** Ityn *Lebek, Parsons, Marcovich* : etin P | Progne *Lebek, Parsons* (Procne), *Marcovich* : prigne P | dum *Marcovich* (*cf. v.*80) : et P | quem *Hutchinson* | colligit P : concinit *Lebek* : contigit *Tandoi* | ilia cruda *Marcovich* : illa cruentus P : illa (ipsa *Parsons*) cruentum *Lebek, Parsons* || **70, 69** : *huic illum versum praeposuit Parsons* || **70** quecumque P | tegit <ca>eli v<i>s *Lebek* (*coll. Ovidii Met.* 1.26) : legit illius P : gerit *Hutchinson et* tellus *Parsons* | *ante* vel *addunt* <mare> *Hutchinson, Nisbet* || **69** cedunt labuntur *A. Dihle* (*ob gradationem*) : labuntur cedunt *Lebek, Parsons, Marcovich* : labunturprecedunt P : labuntur pereunt *Nisbet* ||

(60) "The Father of the universe himself, they say, was buried and gone: he changed his place and went down to visit the infernal realm of his brother. Bacchus perished—so the story goes—through the guile of the Titans, and both Ceres and Venus crossed the stream of death."

(64) "Why should I grieve for a son who is claimed by his destiny? Why should I be exempt from mourning when other mothers mourned in the past? Why, Diomede lost her son, and Agave tore hers asunder. Althaea killed her son, and so did the goddess Ino. Procne too bewailed Itys while collecting his bleeding entrails. For whatever lives under the heavenly ether and the roaming air passes away, perishes, dies, and is buried forever."

60 pater mundi : *Avienus Phaenom*, 21 | tumulatus : *Cicero N.D.* 3.53; *Callim. In Iovem* 8 *sq.*; *Tatian. Oratio* 27; *Athenagoras Legatio* 30; *Clemens Protrept.* 37.4 *et alibi* || **60-63** ... abisse | ... obisse | ... perisse | ... subisse | : *Verg. Aen.* 4.603-606; *C.L.E.* 500.4-7; *A.L.* 273 (*Modestinus*).5-11 || **61** fratri<s> Stygii : *Verg. Aen.* 9.104 *et* 10.113 || **62** *Clemens Protr.* 17.2; *Arnob. Adv. nat.* 5.19 || **63** vadum lethi : *Lucret.* 5.1232; *C.L.E.* 436.14 | Cererem : *Verg. Georg.* 1.39; *Clemens Protr.* 17.1; *Hygin. Fab.* 251; *Orphic. Hymn.* 41.5; *Suda, s.v.* βάραθρον *et alibi* | Veneremque : *Aristides Apologia* 11.3 || **64** fata reposcunt | : *Propert.* 2.1.71; *Ovid. Met.* 13.180 || **68** flevit Ityn Progne : *Horat. Carm.* 4.12.5 *sq.*; *Martialis* 10.51.4; *Ovid. Amores* 3.12.32 || ilia cruda : *Ovid. Fasti* 6.158; *Martialis* 11.57.4; *Livius* 29.27.5; *Statius Silvae* 5.2.115 || **70** <ca>eli v<i>s : *Ovid. Met.* 1.26 | vagus aër : *Tibull.* 3.7.21 ||

Coniugis ut talis vidit Pelieïa fletus,
"Me, <me> trade neci; me, coniux, trade sepulcris,"
exclamat. "Concedo libens, ego tempora dono,
Admete, <e>ventura tibi, pro coniuge coniux.

75 Si vinco matrem, vinco pietate parentem,
si m<or>ior, laus magna mei post funera nostra.
Non ero, sed factum totis narrabitur annis,
et coniux pia semper ero. Non tristior atros
aspiciam vultus, nec toto tempore flebo,

80 dum cineres servabo tuos. Lacrimosa recedat
vita procul: mors ista placet. Me trade sepulcris,
me portet melius nigro velamine Po<r>t<h>meus.

---

71 Pelieïa *Hutchinson* : peleide *P* : pelia edita *Lebek* : Pelieida *Tandoi* || **72** *ante primum* me *notam personae* χ *atque* alcestis *addit P in mg. sinistra* | me <me> *Hutchinson, Parsons (coll. Vergilio)* | *post primum* me *addit* inquid *P, del. Hutchinson, Parsons* : inquit *Ed.* | neci *Lebek, Marcovich* : niquid *P* : inquit *Ed.*, *Oxonienses* | sepolcris *P* || **73** exclamat *Lebek (coll. v.123)* : exclamans *P, retinent Oxonienses* | libiens *P* || **74** <e>ventura *Nisbet* : uentura *P* || **75** si *P* : si<c> *Lebek, Nisbet* | parentem [*i.q.* patrem] *Hutchinson, Nisbet, Marcovich* : parentis *P, retinet Lebek ("die Eltern")* || **76** m<or>ior *Lebek, Hutchinson, Marcovich* : meor *P* : m<or>iar *Ed.* | mei *P* : mihi *Nisbet* | funera nostra *Ed.* : funerenostro *P* : funera restat *Nisbet* : funera constat *Watt* || **78** tristior atros *Ed.* : trustioratrus *P* : tristis *Nisbet et* amatos *Hutchinson* || **79** uultus *P* : cultus *Nisbet* | nec *Marcovich* : non *P* || **80** dum *Marcovich, Watt* : aut *P* (*cf. v.*68) | recedat *Lebek, Hutchinson, Nisbet* : recedam *P* || **81** procum *P* | traderepulcris *P, corr. Ed.* || **82** po<r>t<h>meus *Parsons*, po<r>tmeus *Lebek* : potneus *P* ||

(71) When the daughter of Pelias saw these tears of her husband, she cried aloud: "I, <I> want to be sent to death! My husband, I want to go to the grave for you! I grant you gladly, I donate my coming days to you, Admetus—a spouse for her spouse! If I die for you, if my sense of duty proves to be greater than that of your mother, than that of your father, immense glory will be in store for me after my death. True, I shall be no more, but my feat will be remembered through centuries to come, and I shall live forever as a pious wife. And besides, I shall not look at the sullen faces around me for the rest of my life; I shall not weep each time I attend to your ashes. May such a life of tears stay away from me! I prefer this death. Let me be sent to the grave, let me be carried away by the Carrier attired in black!''

---

72 me, <me> ... me : *Verg. Aen.* 9.427; 8.144 *sq.*; 12.260 *sq.* | trade neci : *Verg. Georg.* 4.90; *Ovid. Fasti* 4.840; *Heroid.* 14.125 | trade sepulcris | : *C.L.E.* 537.4; *Claudian. De Raptu Pros.* 2.251 *sq.* || **74** pro coniuge coniux | : *Ovid. Met.* 7.589 *sq.*; 11.660; *Heroid.* 3.37 || **75** vinco pietate parentem | : *Statius Silvae* 2.1.96; *Silius* 16.474 | pietate : *cf. Eurip. Alc.* 180-182; 338 *sq.*; 641-647; 696 *sq.*; 717; *Plato Sympos.* 179 *c* 1 || **76** laus magna mei : *cf. Eurip. Alc.* 623 *sq.*; *Alcesta* 154 [= *Verg. Aen.* 7.2 *et* 9.249] | funera nostra : *Propert.* 2.1.55 *sq.* || **77** totis narrabitur annis | : *Ovid. Met.* 14.435; *Statius Silvae* 3.2.135 || **78** coniux pia : *Ovid. Met.* 13.301; *Seneca Troades* 501; *C.L.E.* 557.1 *et alibi* || **79** toto tempore flebo | : *Ovid. Pont.* 3.1.103 || **82** portet... Po<r>t<h>meus : *C.L.E.* 1223.7 | nigro velamine : *Ovid. Met.* 11.611 ||

P 160a   Hoc tantum moritura | rogo, ne post mea fata
            dulcior ulla tibi, vestigia ne mea coniux
85   carior ista legat. Et tu, ne<c> nomine tantum,
            me cole, meque puta tecum sub nocte iacere.
            In gremio cineres nostros dignare tenere,
            nec timida tractare manu, sudare fa<v>il<l>as
            unguento, titulumque novo pr<a>ecingere flore.
90   Si redeunt umbr<a>e, veniam tecum<que> iacebo.
            Qualiscumque tamen, coniux, ne desera<r> a te,
            nec doleam de me, quod vitam desero pro te.

---

84 tibi *P* : adeat *Hutchinson* | uestigiam *P* | mea, coniux, *interpungit Lebek* ("*Gatte!*") ||
85 legat *Lebek, Marcovich* : tegat *P, Oxonienses* | ne<c> *Nisbet* : me *P* || **87** cineres *Lebek*
(*cf. v.*80) : cineris *P* | dignare tenere *Lebek, Parsons* : neuedignaretinere [*i.e.*, neve digna
retinere] *P* || **88** tractrare *P* | sudare fa<v>il<l>as | unguento *Lebek, Marcovich* :
sudarefailasunguentum *P* : stillare (*Hutchinson*) favillis (*Ed.*) unguentum *Oxonienses* || **89**
titolumque *P* | precingere *P* || **90** [[de]]re̍déunt *P* | umbre *P* | veniam tecum<que>
{sub nocte} iacebo *Hutchinson, Marcovich* (*cf. v.*86) : ueniam tecum sub nocte iacebo *P*
{veniam} tecum sub nocte iacebo *Ed., Lebek* || **91** -quae *P* | desera<r> *Ed.* : desere
P || *versum* **92** *ante v.*91 *transponit Hutchinson, tum* ne doleas *Parsons, Nisbet* || **92** quid *P*
| desero *Lebek, Nisbet* : degero *P* ||

(83) ''Before I die, I have only one wish for you. After I am gone, may you never love another woman as much as you did me; may the wife to take my place never be dearer to your heart than I have been! As for you, keep loving me! I mean it, not in name only! Think that you are sleeping with me during the night! Do not hesitate to take my ashes into your lap, to caress them with a firm hand! Take care that the urn with my ashes always sweats with oil, and gird my tombstone with fresh flowers! If it is true that shades return, I shall come to lie down with you. Whatever shape I may have then, my husband, abandon me not! Let me never regret my leaving the daylight for you!''

---

83 | hoc tantum : *Silius* 6.501 *sq.* | moritura rogo : *Eurip. Alc.* 299 *sq.*; 308; *Alcesta* 124 [= *Verg. Aen.* 12.816 *et* 3.436] || **84** vestigia ne mea... legat : *Verg. Aen.* 9.392 *sq.*; *Ovid. Met.* 3.17 *et saepius* || **84-85** coniux | carior : *cf. Eurip. Alc.* 181; *Propert.* 5.11.85-90 || **86** tecum sub nocte iacere : *Eurip. Alc.* 350-352; *Ovid. Heroid.* 13.154 || **87** in gremio cineres nostros : *Ovid. Heroid.* 13.157; *Eurip. Alc.* 348-352; *Propert.* 4.11.82 *sq.* || **88** tractare manu : *cf. v.*118; *Statius Silvae* 5.1.87 *sq.*; *Theb.* 4.450; 11.658 || **88-89** sudare fa<v>il<l>as | unguento : *Ovid. Fasti* 3.561; *C.L.E.* 1256.4-6 || **89** novo pr<a>ecingere flore : *C.L.E.* 451.3; 492.20 *sq.*; 578.2; 1036.9 *sq.* || **90** si redeunt umbr<a>e : *Propert.* 4.7.89 | veniam tecum<que> iacebo : *Propert.* 4.7.1-4 || **91** | qualiscumque tamen : *Propert.* 1.18.31; 3.1.30; 3.21.16; 3.23.9 *et alibi* ||

34   TEXT

ANTE OMNES COMMENDO TIBI PIA PIGNORA NATOS,
PIGNORA, QUAE SOLO DE TE FECUNDA CREAVI,
95   EX TE SIC NULLAS HABE＜A＞T MORS ISTA QUERELLAS.
NON PEREO, NEC ENIM MORIOR: ME, CREDE, RESERVO,
QUAE MIHI TAM SIMILES NATOS MORITURA RELINQUO.
QUOS, ROGO, NE PARVOS MAN＜U＞S INDIGNA＜NDA＞ NOVERCAE
PRODAT, ET ＜H＞EU FLENTES MATRIS PIA VINDICET UMBRA.
100 SI TIBI DISSIMULER, SI NON MEA DULCIS IMAGO
PAULUM AD TE VENI＜AT＞...
        ... ET TU PRO CONIUGE CARA
P 160b DISCE MORI, DE M＜E＞ DISCE EXEMPLU＜M＞ | PIETATIS.''

---

93 omnes *Nisbet, Marcovich (coll. Vergilio)* : omnem *P* || **95** ex *Marcovich* : de *P* (*cf. vv.*62 *et* 103) | te *P* : me *Shackleton Bailey* | habe＜a＞t *Lebek, Parsons, Marcovich* : habet *P* | quae-[[.]]rellam *P* || **96** pereor *P* | moreor *P* | me crede reseruo *P* : mi crede, reservo＜r＞ *Ed., agn. Oxonienses* || **97** mihi *Nisbet* : tibi *P, defendit Koenen* || **98** mans *P* | indigna＜nda＞ *R. Kassel* : indigna *P* : ＜ulla＞ indigna *Watt* : ＜umquam＞ indigna *Tandoi* || **99** prodat, et ＜h＞eu *Marcovich* : proderentet *P* : proderet et *Ed., agn. Lebek* : prodiderit *Tandoi* : verberet et *Nisbet* : proterat et *Watt* || **100** si tibi dissimuler *M. von Albrecht et* si *Marcovich* : si tibi dissimiles hoc *P* : si mihi dissimiles, si *Hutchinson* | dulcis | simago *P* || **101** paulum *P* : rursum *Nisbet* | ad te *Marcovich* : nạte *sive* nọte *P* : no⟨c⟩te *Ed.*: nota *Parsons* | veni⟨at⟩ *Marcovich*: ueni *P* : veni＜t＞ *Lebek, Parsons (sine lacuna)* | *post* veni＜at＞ *lacunam, uxoris oblitae vindictam continentem, statuit Marcovich (cf. Verg. Aen.* 4.386) || **102** cara *Nisbet, Marcovich* : caro *P, retinet Lebek* [*i.e.,* "et tu, lector, pro coniuge caro"] || **103** de m＜e＞ disce exemplu＜m＞ *Nisbet (cf. Sil. Pun.* 5.636-639) : disceexmexempla *P* : ＜tu＞ disce exempla ex m＜e＞ *Hutchinson* : disce＜s＞ ex me＜e＞ exemplum *Watt* ||

(93) "And before anything else, I entrust you with the sacred pledge of our love, our children; the pledge which I have borne being pregnant by you alone, so that you may have no complaint about this (premature) death of mine. I shall not perish, I shall not die: believe me, I am preserving myself by leaving behind me the children resembling their mother so much. They are still young: I beg you, may no unworthy hand of a step-mother betray them! Alas! Know that the faithful shade of the mother will come to avenge her crying children!"

(100) "But if you neglect me, if the sweet image of me does not come to your mind from time to time...

... And you too learn to die for your (new) dear wife (if need be); learn from my example what a sense of duty is!"

---

93 | ante omnes : *Verg. Aen.* 5.406 *et saepius* | commendo tibi pia pignora natos | : *Propert.* 4.11.73 | pia pignora natos | : *Dracont. Romulea* 6.56 || **94** *Propert.* 4.11.36 *et* 68; *C.L.E.* 1038.6; 1306.4 || **95** *C.L.E.* 492.5 *sq.* || **96** *Horat. Carm.* 3.30.6 || **98** man<u>s indigna<nda> novercae : *Eurip. Alc.* 305-310; 372 *sq.*, *Propert.* 4.11.85-90; *Alcesta* 127 *sq.* [= *Verg. Aen.* 4.496 *et* 10.532] || **99** flentes... vindicet : *cf. Stith Thompson, Motif-Index* E221.2.1; E323.2 *et alibi* | pia... umbra | : *Propert.* 3.18.31 || **100** si tibi dissimuler : *Ovid. Pont.* 1.2.146 | dulcis imago | : *Statius Silvae* 1.2.122 *sq.*; *Theb.* 5.608 || **102** et tu : *cf. v.*85 et tu | coniuge cara | : *C.L.E.* 490.3; 452.1 *et saepius* || **103** *Silius* 5.636-639 ||

Iam vaga sideribus Nox pingebatur et ales
105 rore soporifero conpleve<ra>t omnia Somnus:
ad mortem properans, in coniuge fixa iacebat
Alcestis lacrimasq<ue> viri peritura videbat.
Plangere saepe iubet sese natosque virumque,
disponit famulos, conponit in ordine funus
110 l<a>eta sibi: pictosque toros variosque pa<ratus>...
                                    † ... ones †
barbaricas frondes <et> odores, tura crocumque.
Pallida sudanti destringit balsama virga,
ereptum nido percidit pulver amomum,
115 arida purpureis destringit cinnama ramis,
arsurosque omnes secum disponit odores.

---

104 *ante* iam *addit P* poet(a) *in mg. sinistra* | ales *Parsons* : alis *P* || **105** sopordfero *P* | conpleve<ra>t... Somnus *Parsons* : conplebent... somnum *P* || **106** iacabat *P* || **107** alcestem *P* | -q<ue> viri *Lebek, Hutchinson, Nisbet* : quiri *P* || **108** saepe iubet *P* : sed prohibet *Shackleton Bailey* : saepe vetat *F. Jones* || **110** leta *P* | sibi *P* : subit *Watt* | pictusque *P* | *post* variosque *lacunam statuit Hutchinson, post* pa<ratus> *Marcovich* || **110-111** pa<ratus> | † ... ones † *Marcovich* : paones *P* : paratus (*sine lacuna*) *Lebek* : <tapetas> | *Nisbet et* ... <re>ponens | *Parsons* || **112** barbaricas (*corr. ex* uaruar-) *P* : Arabicas *Nisbet* | <et> odores *Lebek, Hutchinson, Nisbet, Marcovich* : oduresque *P* | crucumque *P* || **113** pallida *Parsons, Marcovich* : pallada *P* : Pallada *Lebek* ("Öl *streift sie vom balsamtriefenden Zweig*") | destringit *Lebek* : [[u]]distringit *P* : *corruptum Oxonienses* : destillat *Nisbet* | palsama *P* || **114** percidit *Marcovich* : precidit *P* : pr<a>ecidit *Ed., agn. omnes* | puluer *P* : † puluer † *Oxonienses* : culmen *Nisbet* | amomum *Marcovich* : amomi *P, omnes* || **115** destringit *Lebek, Hutchinson* : distringit *P* (*cf. v.*113) || **116** arsurusque *P* | desponit *P* ||

(104) Stars had already begun to adorn the roving Night, and the winged god of Sleep had already dropped the slumber-bringing dew in everybody's eyes: only Alcestis, hastening to die, was lying awake— gazing at her husband, watching him shed tears at her imminent death. Now, she bids both her husband and her children often to mourn aloud for her; she takes care of her servants in her last will; she arranges for her own funeral with a cheerful heart. Here is her ornate bier (palliasse), here her motley funeral coverlet (apparel)...

(112) ... (she collects) exotic plants, spices and perfumes, frankincense (olibanum) and saffron-essence. She scrapes off the pale balsam-gum from the wet balsam-tree; she beats the amomum to powder, snatched away from a bird's nest; she strips off the dry cinnamon-twigs from their purple-colored boughs; and she gives orders for all these spices to be burnt on the pyre along with her.

104-107 cf. Verg. Aen. 4.522 sq. et 529-531 || 104-105 Verg. Aen. 3.147; 2.8 sq.; 9.224-227 | 104 vaga... Nox : Statius Silvae 3.1.42 | sideribus Nox pingebatur : Seneca Medea 310; Thyest. 834; Manil. 1.445 || 104-105 ales | ... Somnus : A.L. 273.1 (Modestinus); Stat. Theb. 10.302 || 105 rore soporifero : Verg. Aen. 5.854-856; Ovid. Met. 11.586; Lucan. 3.8 sq.; Lucret. 4.453 sq. || 107 lacrimasq<ue> viri : Eurip. Alc. 201; Ovid. Heroid. 10.119-121 || 108 plangere saepe : C.L.E. 682.10; 1036.6 | natosque virumque | : Ovid. Met. 6.301 sq. || 110 pictosque toros : Verg. Aen. 1.708; 4.206 sq.; Ovid. Heroid. 12.30 | variosque pa<ratus> : Tacit. Ann. 13.17.1; Verg. Aen. 6.220-222; Stat. Silvae 2.1.159; Theb. 6.62 sq. || 112 frondes : Verg. Aen. 4.506 sq.; Stat. Theb. 6.54-58 et alibi | tura crucumque : Verg. Georg. 1.56 sq. || 112 tura crocumque, 113 balsama, 114 amomum, 115 cinnama : Stat. Silvae 2.1.159-162; 2.4.34-36; 2.6.86-88; 3.3.33-35; 5.1.210-216; 5.3.41-43; Theb. 6.59-63; Ovid. Met. 10.307-310; Martialis 11.54.1-3 || 113 pallida ... balsama : Plin. N.H. 12.48; 13.17; Ovid. Met. 15.399; Stat. Silvae 3.2.141 | sudanti... virga | : Verg. Georg. 2.118 sq.; Stat. Silvae 3.2.141; Prudent. Cathemerinon 5.117-119 et alibi || 114 ereptum nido : Plin. N.H. 12.85; Herodot. 3.111 | pulver amomum : Ovid. Trist. 3.3.69; Plin. N.H. 12.49 ||

<H>ora propinquabat lucem ra<p>tura puellae,
tractavitque manu: rigor omnia corripiebat.
C<a>eruleos ungues oculis moritura notabat

120 algentisque pedes, fatali frigore pressos.
Admeti in gremiu<m> refugit fugientis imago. |

P 161a   Ut vidit sensus <labi>, "Dulcissime coniux,"
exclamat, "rapior: venit, mors ultima venit,
infernusque deus claudit <mea> membra sopore."

---

117 ora *P* | ratura *P* || **118** tractavitque manu [*sc.* Hora mortis] *Marcovich* (*cf. v.*88) : tractabatquaemanos *P* : tractabatque manus *Ed.* : attrectansque *vel* frigebantque manus *Nisbet* : *corruptum Oxonienses* : torpebantque manus *Watt, Tandoi* | omnia [*sc.* membra: *cf. v.*105: omnia *sc.* animalia] *P* : extima *Nisbet* | corripiebat *Nisbet* : diripiebat *P* : praeripiebat *Hutchinson* || **119** ceruleos *P* | oculos *P, corr. Ed.* | moritura *P* (*cf. vv.* 83, 97, 107) : moribunda *Nisbet* || **120** pressos *Hutchinson, Marcovich* : pressum *P* : pressa *Parsons* : prensos *Nisbet* : pressam *Lebek* || **121** admeti *P* (*cf. vv.*4 et 74) : coniugis *Hutchinson* | gremiu<m> *Hutchinson* : gremio *P, retinet Lebek* | *post* imago *addit P* ∫∫ >— alcestis *in mg. dextra* || **122** uidit *P* : cedit *coni. Hutchinson* : perdit *Watt* | sensus : *in P litterae* nsus *lineola transfixae esse videntur* | <labi> *add. Hutchinson* | *ante* dulcissime *repetit P* coniux e[[.]]x : *ut dissographiam del. Ed.* || **123** rapeor *P* | moris *P* || **124** inferuusque *P* | claudit *Lebek, Hutchinson, Nisbet, Marcovich* : claudet *P* : condit *coni. Hutchinson, Nisbet, Parsons* | <mea> *suppl. Ed.* : *vacat spatium trium litt. in P* : <mihi> *suppl. Hutchinson* | sembra soporem *P, corr. Ed.* ||

(117) The Hour of death started approaching the young woman to take away her daylight. She touched her with her hand, no more: numbness began seizing her every limb. Dying slowly, she watched her fingernails turning blue, her freezing feet growing heavy with the frost of death. A fleeting shadow (woman no more), she seeks refuge in Admetus' lap. And when she felt that her senses < were leaving her for good >, she cries aloud: ''Husband, my love! Death, death at the last has come: she is taking me away. The infernal god is enfolding < my > limbs with slumber.''

117 <H>ora : *C.I.L.* V.6710; *C.L.E.* 55.7; 389.2; 1295.3 | propinquabat : *Alcesta* 46 [= *Verg. Aen.* 12.150] *et* 54 [= *Aen.* 9.355]; *Statius Achill.* 1.257 *sq.*; *Tac. Ann.* 6.28; *Verg. Aen.* 2.730 *et saepius* | lucem ra<p>tura : *C.L.E.* 466.3 || **118** tractavitque manu : *Verg. Aen.* 10.419; *C.L.E.* 995.8; *supra v.*88 | rigor omnia corripiebat : *Silius* 4.455 *sq*; *Alcesta* 133 [= *Aen.* 4.499]|| **119** c<a>eruleos ungues : *Epicedion Drusi* 93 || **120** algentisque pedes : *Seneca Nat. Quaest.* 4.5.3 | fatali frigore pressos : *Lucret.* 6.845; *Ovid. Ars Amat.* 2.317; *Pont.* 1.7.11; *Silius* 5.527-529; 6.170; *Ovid. Heroid.* 9.135 *sq.* || **121** in gremiu<m> : *Verg. Georg.* 2.326; *Lucan.* 8.106; *Lucret.* 1.33 *sq.*; *Verg. Aen.* 8.405 *sq.*; *Tibull.* 1.1.59 *sq.*; *C.L.E.* 1138.2 | fugientis imago | : *Verg. Aen.* 10.656; *Silius* 17.644 || **122** sensus <labi> : *Verg. Aen.* 11.818 *sq.*; *Statius Theb.* 8.734 *sq.*; *Eurip. Alc.* 203 | dulcissime coniux | : *C.L.E.* 542.4; 1139.1; 1338.1; 1436.3; *C.I.L.* IX.6417.5 *et saepius* || **123** mors ultima venit : *Lucilius Iunior ap Sen. Epist.* 24.21; *Eurip. Alc.* 259 *sq.*; *Alcesta* 161 [= *Aen.* 6.46] || **124** infernusque deus : *Verg. Aen.* 6.106; *Ovid. Met.* 2.261; *Eurip. Alc.* 268 | membra sopore | : *Lucret.* 4.453 *sq.*; *Verg. Aen.* 8.406; *Silius* 3.170; *C.L.E.* 481.3; *Seneca Herc. Oet.* 534; *Lucan.* 9.671; *Propert.* 3.11.54 ||

COMMENTARY

1-11. *Admetus consults Apollo*

The poet follows the pattern of a Greek/Roman prayer: (1) *Invocatio* (1-2); (2) Request (3-9); finally, (3) "the binding formula" (9-11). But the point is that, in this poem, all three elements are exaggerated. Admetus' *epiclesis* opens with a salvo of five divine epithets (with a sixth one hiding in the lacuna of line 3). This may sound pompous, but the poet seems to be conveying the old hymnodic idea of πολυώνυμος ὁ θεός (compare Karl Keyssner, *Gottesvorstellung und Lebensauffassung im griechischen Hymnus* [Würzburger Studien zur Altertumswissenschaft, 21], Stuttgart, 1932, 46 ff.). In other words, the consultant is trying to say: "O god, hear me, with *whatever* name you like to be called!" Compare Plato *Crat.* 400 e 1: ὥσπερ ἐν ταῖς εὐχαῖς νόμος ἐστὶν ἡμῖν εὔχεσθαι, οἵτινές τε καὶ ὁπόθεν χαίρουσιν [sc. οἱ θεοὶ] ὀνομαζόμενοι, ταῦτα καὶ ἡμᾶς αὐτοὺς καλεῖν, ὡς ἄλλο μηδὲν εἰδότας; Aeschylus *Agam.* 160-162: Ζεύς, ὅστις ποτ᾽ ἐστίν, εἰ τόδ᾽ αὐ- | τῷ φίλον κεκλημένῳ, | τοῦτό νιν προσεννέπω (and Ed. Fraenkel ad loc.).

It is, however, equally possible that Admetus' invocation is grandiloquent because his request is an unusual one. He wants to learn from Apollo three different things: (1) the length of his life-span or the exact day of his death (3 f.: *da scire diem, da noscere, quando...*); (2) the very cause of his death (5 *quae finis vitae*); finally, (3) what will happen to his own *self* (*ego*) after the death (5 f.: *qui<d> mi post fata relinquant...*). Only the first request is relevant to the Alcestis-myth, the other two are one of many expansions of the Barcelona bard. But the point is that no mortal man is supposed to know any of these three things. My explanation is that the poet deliberately wanted to present Admetus as too self-confident, arrogant, and lacking in *religious wisdom*, as a *foil* to the *pietas* of his noble spouse.

Admetus is well aware of the fact that his request is an unusual one. That is why he feels it necessary to *urge* Apollo—(3) *da scire diem, da noscere, quando*; (5) *quae..., qui<d>*; (6) *edoce*; finally, (9) *ede tamen*. And that is why his "binding formula" is a powerful one, consisting of four elements—(9) *si te colui*; (10) | *succepi*; (11) | *accepi*; finally, (11) *iussi* ("Tell me, if I *worshiped* you ever; if I ever gave you *shelter* when you came to me as a terrified servant after the gods' charge against you; if I ever *accepted* you to be my herdsman, and I myself *sent* you to the forests to raise shouts of joy!"). All four elements—Admetus' special worship of Apollo; his offer of a shelter and acceptance of the god as a herdsman;

finally, Admetus' generosity with his divine servant—may be paralleled in the traditional myth (with the only exception of the obvious poetic exaggeration, 9 *paventem*, "as a terrified servant"). But the point is that our poet makes Admetus mention all this to Apollo to *bind* the god—*do, ut des*.

In conclusion, Admetus' request is either hubristic or arrogant, and attests to his lack in religious wisdom and to his foolishness.

1. Pr<a>escie Lauripotens : Apparently, *praescius* is to be found nowhere in Latin poetry as an epithet of Apollo. J. B. Carter, *Epitheta deorum* etc. (Leipzig, 1902), lists under *praescius*: Carmentis, Iuno, Manto, Themis, and Thetis alone. The closest expression to our lines 1-2 seems to be Claudian *De Raptu Proserpinae* 2.109: *venturi praescia laurus* |. For *praescia* opening a line compare: Verg. *Aen.* 6.66 = Ovid *Met.* 13.162; Lucan 2.3; Claudian *Carm. min.* 30.16.—**Lauripotens** as an epithet of Apollo occurs only in Martianus Capella 1.24. Probably its rarity was the reason for a glossographer to add the supralinear gloss in the exemplar of P—*apollo. Lauripotens* is of significance here, since it is leading to the expression of line 2: *invoco te laurusque...*

Latonie with Apollo is to be found only in Hostius, and there in company of *Arquitenens* (cf. v.3): *invictus Apollo* | *arquitenens Latonius* (*Poet.* 4 [6] Morel, ap. Macrob. *Sat.* 6.5.8).—Notice the hymnodic alliteration of the invocation (1-2): P LP L D P | L L.

2. invoco te laurusque : The invocation of the laurels along with Apollo may suggest that the poet is envisaging Admetus as consulting the Apollo Pythius at Delphi. If so, then the expression of line 21, *Ille larem post dicta petit*, would mean that Admetus, after consulting Apollo at Delphi, returns home to Pherae in Thessaly. In addition, the expression of line 2, "I invoke you along with the laurels," may well hint at the old belief that Apollo likes to *hide* in a laurel tree (compare Apollo Δαφναῖος, Δαφνίτης). That is the reason why we read in the Homeric Hymn to Apollo (395 f.): "Whatever Apollo may speak in answer from his laurel tree" (ὅττι κεν εἴπῃ | χρείων ἐκ δάφνης), and why the first temple at Delphi was made of laurel trees only (Pausanias 10.5.5). One should never forget the fact that the Barcelona bard is extremely well versed in mythology.— | **invoco** : This is the preferred position of the form: cf., e.g., | *invocat* Verg. *Aen.* 7.140; Ovid *Met.* 10.640; 11.562; 13.561; *Ars Amat.* 3.376; Propert. 3.15.22; Stat. *Theb.* 9.162; Valer. Fl. 2.364; Claudian *Carm. min.* 28.4

lectas : Apollo's sacred laurel is *select* among the trees, it is a *choice* tree. P seems to offer [[*t*]]*cectas* [i.e., *tectas* corrected into *cectas*]. I read *lectas*, first, because our scribe confounds *t* and *l* also in lines 70 (*legit* for *tegit*) and 85 (*tegat* for *legat*); and second, because of the hymnodic alliteration in *epiclesis*—*Lauripotens, Latonie, laurusque... lectas*.

3. <Arcitenens> : The ousted original word must have been another epithet of Apollo, to justify the presence of the supralinear explanatory gloss *apollo* (just as in line 1, the supralinear gloss *apollo* explains its rare epithet *lauripotens* in P). Metrically, *Arcitenens* seems to be the best candidate: it is employed in this position by Hostius first (quoted ad v.1), by Corippus *Iohannis* 1.458 last, and it appears in company of *Latonius* (as here) in Hostius. The epithet is frequent enough: Naevius *Poet.* 30 (32).1 Morel; Accius *Trag.* 167 Ribbeck; Verg. *Aen.* 3.75; Ovid *Met.* 1.441; 6.265; Silius 5.177; Stat. *Achill.* 1.682; *Silvae* 4.4.95; Arnob. *Adv. nat.* 1.36 and 4.22; Sidonius Apollinaris *Carm.* 1.7 and 23.266. Finally, *Arcitenens* might have formed an alliteration with (4) *Admeti fatalia* and (6) *animus... in auras*.

diem : i.e., *diem fatalem sive mortis*. Compare v.26: *Me rapit, ecce, dies*; *Alcesta* [*A.L.* I, No. 15 Riese] 53 f.: | *Disce tuum...* | *advenisse diem* [= Verg. *Aen.* 12.146 and 7.145]; 82 *stat sua cuique dies* [= *Aen.* 10.467]; *C.L.E.* 1522.15 Buecheler: *die sua peremptus*; Apollodor. *Bibl.* 1.9.15.3.

4. Admeti : The speaker identifies himself for the benefit of the reader (following an old convention of Greek tragedy).

fatalia fila : I am unable to parallel the expression. My guess is that it is a combination of Ovid *Pont.* 1.8.64: *nerunt fatales fortia fila deae* and *C.L.E.* 436.8 f.: *Parcae* | *et nevere super vobis vitalia fila*.

fila Sorores | (= v.27 **Parcae**) : This is a trite clausula: Lucan 6.703; Silius 3.96; 17.361; Stat. *Silvae* 1.4.123; *C.L.E.* 443.4 f.: *Clotho* | *et favit rupisse suas quoque fila sorores*; 456.4; 1011.5; 1114.4: | *cum mea Lethaeae ruperunt fila sorores*; (Martial 11.36.3 f.).

5. quae finis vitae : As already stated, the poet expands the traditional myth by making Admetus ask Apollo—in addition to the *length* of his life-span—about the very *cause* of his death, and about the *future* of his "self" (*ego*) after the death.—*finis vitae* : Accius *Trag.* 451; Seneca *Phaedra* 670; Lucret. 3.943; 3.1093; Ovid *Ibis* 312: *quem finem vitae Sardanapallus habet*.

qui<d> mi : Evidently, this *mi* is opposed to *animus* of the following line: "Tell me, what Destiny may have in store *for me* once *my spirit* has gone into the starry sphere." That is to say, Admetus has no doubt that, after his death, his *soul* will ascend to the heavenly realm of *Sternenbereich*: what he actually wants to learn from the prescient Apollo is what will happen to his *own self* (*quid mi*)—probably, to his shadow (εἴδωλον) preserving its bodily shape. Will it be allowed to go to "the islands of the blessed" (this may be implied by the expression of line 7: *ni prospera vita futura* <*est*>), or Destiny would rather send it to the gloomy realm of

Acheron, to the *pallida regna* (8), anticipating *Acherontis... regna* (of line 13 f.), and *fratri*<*s*> *Stygii regnum* (of line 61).

Now, such an eschatological distinction between *ego* and *meus animus*, between my shade (εἴδωλον) and my soul (ψυχή), is difficult to parallel in Greek and Roman folklore. How different such an idea is from the common sentiment, expressed, for example, in *C.L.E.* 1366.3 f.:

> Exacto vitae transcendit ad aethera cursu,
>   terrenum tumulo dans, animam superis.

My explanation is that—here as elsewhere else (vv. 32-35; 40-42; 51 f.; 90; 117-124)—our poet is being carried away by his vivid imagination in combining two beliefs incompatible with each other.

mi post fata relinquant | : Ovid *Met.* 14.153: *vocem mihi fata relinquent.* |

6. siderea<**s**>**... auras** : Cf. Verg. *Aen.* 3.585 f.: *aethra* | *siderea*; Seneca *Herc. Oet.* 893: *auras... caelestes.*

animus quando ivit in auras | : Ovid *Heroid.* 10.121: *spiritus infelix peregrinas ibit in auras*; *Trist.* 1.5.11 f.: *spiritus et vacuas prius hic tenuandus in auras* | *ibit.* P has *luit*, which I would read *ivit*. This perfect tense is rare in poetry (Dracontius *Orestes* 447). Still, I think a perfect tense is needed here to serve as an antecedent to, *qui*<*d*> *mi post fata relinquant*, of line 5: "Tell me, what Destiny may have in store for me *once* my spirit *has gone* into the starry sphere." In addition, *luit* is closer to *iuit* than to *ibit*. In view of the two instances of *ibit* to Ovid, however, this reading in our text as well cannot be ruled out. Of course, *post* in v.5 is an adverb, and *quando* in v.6 is relative.

7. ni : P has *sit*, which may be explained either as a dittography of *sit* in the next line, or as a remnant of <*ni*>*si* (compare *nihil* in lines 36 and 40, for *nil*). The sense, however, requires *ni*: "It is anguish for a man to know his future after the death, *unless* it is going to be a *blessed life*."

prospera vita : Cf. Lucan 8.625: *fata tibi longae fluxerunt prospera vitae*; 8.631 f.: *mutantur prospera vitā,* | *non fit morte miser*. The expression, "a prosperous life", as referring to the life *after death*, sounds as little convincing as does the expression, *fugientis imago* (121), as referring to the dying Alcestis. Probably, we are dealing with a young poet.

8. sit<**ne**> : This seems to be the best means to introduce a parenthetic clause: "Is it going to be a life without light, a realm of shadows?" Another interrogative -*ne* has been dropped by our scribe in line 59: *Non*<*ne*>.

atra dies : In Latin poetry, it usually means, *dies suprema* or *mortis* (cf. *Oxford Latin Dictionary*, s.v. *ater*, 6b): Verg. *Aen.* 6.429; 11.28; Propert. 2.11.4; Valer. Fl. 5.41; Silius 5.591; Stat. *Theb.* 3.636; 8.376; *C.L.E.* 1036.2; 1262.4; 1385.12; 1401.2: *sustulit atra dies* |. Our poet, however, employs the expression as a hendiadys with *pallida regna*: "the life after death in the gloomy Hades." Such an innovation fails to convince.

pallida regna | : Silius 11.472; 13.408; Verg. *Aen.* 8.244 f.; Lucan 1.456; Arator *Acta apostol.* 1.179.—In addition to these instances, *regna* is the most likely reading here in view of the expressions, *Acherontis... regna* (13 f.), and *fratri* < *s* > *Stygii regnum* (61). P offers *uitam* instead, probably under the influence of *uita* in the preceding line. The reading *vita* is highly unlikely to me, since *dies* implies here "life," so that the expression, *pallida vita*, would be a tedious repetition after *atra dies*, in the same line. It is a golden rule in palaeography that the last word of a verse is most frequently being damaged. P is no exception to this rule, while offering: 25 *sororum* | (for *suorum* |); 37 *uitam* (?) | (for *vis iam* |); 39 *ullam* | (for *una* |); 66 *acatem* | (for *Agaue* |); 67 *ion* | (for *Ino* |); 110 *pa* | (for *pa* < *ratus* > |).

9. si te colui : Admetus' piety with Apollo is well established: Eurip. *Alc.* 10 f. (Apollo speaking): ὁσίου γὰρ ἀνδρὸς ὅσιος ὢν ἐτύγχανον | παιδὸς Φέρητος; 23: λείπω μελάθρων τῶνδε φιλτάτην στέγην. Statius *Theb.* 6.374 (Apollo of Admetus and Amphiaraus): *ambo pii carique ambo*; 377: *tura dabat famulo* (sc. Admetus to Apollo).

10. | **succepi... 11** | **accepi** : Compare 66 | *amisit...* 67 | *perdidit...* 68 | *flevit...*; 84 | *dulcior...* 85 | *carior...*, and the chain of rhymes in lines 60-63.

pecudumque ducem : Cf. *Culex* 175: *ducem gregis* (i.q. *pastorem*); Tibull. 1.10.10.

post crimina divum : "after the gods' charges against you:" Cf. Eurip. *Alc.* 6 f.: καί με θητεύειν πατὴρ | θνητῷ παρ' ἀνδρὶ τῶνδ' ἄποιν' ἠνάγκασεν; Statius *Theb.* 6.375-378 (Apollo speaking of Admetus):

> Peliacis hic cum famularer in arvis
> (sic Iovis imperia et nigrae volvere Sorores),
> tura dabat famulo nec me sentire minorem
> ausus.

Lucian *De sacrif.* 4: κἀξοστρακισθεὶς διὰ τοῦτο ἐκ τοῦ οὐρανοῦ (sc. Apollo)...; et alibi.—*crimina divum* | : Cf. Lucan 5.59: *crimenque deorum* |; Seneca *Controv. excerpta* 10.5: *deorum crimina in templis picta sunt*.

11. iussi < **que** > **idem** : Cf. Hyginus *Fab.* 51.2: *Apollo autem, quod ab eo* (sc. Admeto) *in servitudinem liberaliter esset acceptus*,...; Stat. *Theb.* 6.377 f.: *nec me sentire minorem* | *ausus*.

dare iubila silvis : The whoop and halloo of the shepherds sometimes implies the sense of freedom and joy in pastoral poetry. Compare Calpurn. *Ecl.* 1.30 and 7.3; Silius 14.475; *T.L.L.* VII.588.60-69.—*Silvis* is ablative (for *in silvis*), since shepherds usually raise shouts to *call* each other, not to produce an echo with the trees.

12-20. *Apollo gives a surprise answer*

In contrast to Admetus' emotional request (filled with anaphoras), Apollo's unexpected answer is unadorned and down to earth (cf. 12: *doleo, sed vera fatebo*<r>). Plutarch's words (*De Pythiae oraculis* 397 B) come to mind: Σίβυλλα δὲ μαινομένῳ στόματι καθ' Ἡράκλειτον [B 92 DK = 75 Marcovich] ἀγέλαστα καὶ ἀκαλλώπιστα καὶ ἀμύριστα φθεγγομένη χιλίων ἐτῶν ἐξικνεῖται τῇ φωνῇ διὰ τὸν θεόν. Compare also Introduction, p. 6. Apollo's answer boils down to two things: (1) Your day of death is imminent. (2) However, a substitute victim, coming from a member of Admetus' family (one of his small children being not excluded), will be agreeable to the Fates (*Parcae* of line 27). Now, just as in lines 5-9 (*quae finis vitae, qui* < d > *mi post fata relinquant...*), here too our poet expands the traditional myth by introducing the folkloric motif of "the tantamount life-span:" *tu poteris posthac alieno vivere fato* (17).

12. Pr<a>escius <h>eu P<a>ean : The epithet seems to echo Admetus' confident invocation in the opening line: *Pr<a>escie... P<a>ean*, with a probable ironical sneer, on the part of Apollo: "You wanted to know (what no mortal man is supposed to know), you insisted (3: *da scire diem, da noscere, quando*; 5: *quae finis vitae, qui* < d > *mi...*; 6: *edoce*; finally, 9: *ede tamen*). Well, I will tell you, but you will regret (12: <h>*eu*) your curiosity!" If so, then Apollo is witnessing to Admetus' hubristic requests.

sed vera fatebo<r> | : Statius *Achill.* 1.146; Ovid *Heroid.* 8.97; cf. 14.47; *Pont.* 3.1.79; 3.9.19.

13. mors vicina premit : Lucan 7.50: *mortis vicinae properantes admovet horas*; Seneca *Epist.* 30.7: *cum loqueretur de morte vicina*; *Alcesta* 53 f.: | *disce tuum* [= Verg. *Aen.* 12.146]... | *advenisse diem* [= *Aen.* 7.145]; *nam lux inimica propinquat* [= 9.355].

m<a>estique Ac<h>eron<t>is... regna : Silius 14.243: *ausus adire diem, maestoque Acheronte relicto,...*; cf. *Culex* 273: *maesta... Ditis... regna* |; Lucan 6.782: *Tartara maesta* |.

14. gratam... lucem : Horace *Sat.* 1.5.39: | *Postea lux oritur multo gratissima*; Lucret. 3.935: | *nam* <si> *grata fuit tibi vita*; Claudian 26.308 f.: *hic carior omni* | *luce gener.*

15. mortis damna : The explicative genitive *mortis* sounds redundant, since *damnum* already means *mors* (cf. *T.L.L.* V.26.46-60). For the expression, compare Ulpian *Dig.* 13.6.5.7: *damna mortis*; Ausonius 5.2.31 g.: *quiesce placidus et caduci corporis* | *damnum repende gloria.*

16. possit : i.e., *qui fortitudinem animumque habeat*, "whoever may have the heart to suffer death." Compare Verg. *Aen.* 4.419 f.: *Hunc ego si potui* *tantum sperare dolorem | et perferre, soror, potero*. On the contrary, *tu poteris*, in the next line, means, "you will be able, you will be allowed to." Differently Lebek (21): "Semantisch entwertet: Hofmann-Szantyr, *Lat. Syntax²* 313 f.; 319."

instantis... casus : Cf. *Alcesta* 75: *fatoque urgenti incumbere vellet |* [= *Aen.* 2.653]; *subiti casus*: Ovid *Heroid.* 13.132; *Trist.* 5.1.9; Lucan 6.597 f.; Juvenal 3.273; Quintil. *Inst.* 10.3.3.

17. alieno vivere fato | : The phrase may yield two different senses, depending on whether *fatum* means "death" or rather "destiny". If the former, then the ablative is causal, and the meaning would be, "you will be allowed henceforth to live *thanks* to the death of somebody else." This interpretation may find support in Ovid *Met.* 15.90: *alteriusque animantem animantis vivere leto*. If the latter, then the ablative is, say, instrumental, and the meaning would be, "you will be granted henceforth to live (on) the destiny of somebody else."

Now, although both interpretations are possible, I am inclined toward the latter one for the following reasons. First, the idea of "a substitute *death*" has already been conveyed both by the clause, *pro te qui mortis damna subire | possit*, of line 15, and by the one of line 16, *instantis in se convertere casus*. Consequently, the expression of this line 17, *alieno vivere fato*, in the sense of, "to live because of the death of somebody else," would be redundant. Second, *fatum*, in the sense of "destiny", finds support both in line 20, and particularly in the expression, *tempora donare*, of lines 29 and 73, meaning, "to donate my allotted days to you."

For the expression of 73 f., *tempora <e> ventura donare*, clearly refers to the amount of years allotted by the Fates to Alcestis (and, in line 29, to Pheres), and may explain the phrase of 17, *alieno vivere fato*, "to live the destiny of somebody else." Admetus then would live as many years as would have lived his *vicaria victima*.

If this line of interpretation is correct, then our poet is employing here the folkloric motif of transfer of the years of life of one person to the account of another person. The possibility that the poet had found this motif in a lost version of the Alcestis myth I think cannot be ruled out. For in a *Hypothesis* to Euripides' *Alcestis* we read: Ἀπόλλων ᾐτήσατο παρὰ τῶν Μοιρῶν ὅπως ὁ Ἄδμητος τελευτᾶν μέλλων παράσχῃ τὸν ὑπὲρ ἑαυτοῦ ἑκόντα τεθνηξόμενον, ἵνα ἴσον τῷ προτέρῳ χρόνον ζήσῃ. However, the probability is that the poet had taken over the motif of "tantamount life-span" directly from Latin poetry. Compare Propertius 4.11.95 (Cornelia to Paullus): *quod mihi detractum est, vestros accedat ad annos* (and, as lines 93, 94, and 98 of our poem attest, the *regina elegiarum* was a major source of inspiration for our poet); Ovid *Met.* 7.168 (Jason to Medea): *deme meis annis et demptos adde parenti*; Tibull. 1.6.63 f.: *proprios ego tecum, | sit modo fas, annos contribuisse velim; C.L.E.* 995.13-16 (Atimetus to Homonoea):

Si pensare animas sinerent crudelia fata
    et posset redimi morte aliena salus,
quantulacumque meae debentur tempora vitae,
    pensassem pro te, cara Homonoea, libens.

995.25 f. (Homonoea to Atimetus):

Quodque mihi eripuit mors inmatura iuventae,
    id tibi victuro proroget ulterius.

On the motif itself cf. Stith Thompson, E165; D1855.2; T211.1.

19. | **et coniux natique rudes** : Lucan 4.396: | *iam coniux natique rudes*.

lumina... | **qui claudat** : Compare 14: *gratamque relinquere lucem* and Eurip. *Alc.* 18 θανὼν πρὸ κείνου μηκέτ᾽ εἰσορᾶν φάος.

pro te | : Compare 91 *a te* |, and 92 *pro te* |.

20. fatoque tuo tumuloque : The expression seems to mean, "in place of your fate and grave." If so, then *fatum* here may speak in favor of the same sense in line 17 as well, i.e., "destiny, fate".

21-31. Admetus asks Pheres

With line 21, we most probably move from Delphi to Admetus' royal palace at Pherae in Thessaly (*ille larem post dicta petit*). Now, once at home Admetus does not follow the instruction of Apollo (19: *pete*, "go and ask"), but rather it is his father who comes to see him first (23). This is hardly a stratagem on the part of Admetus, but rather our poet had decided to employ *variatio*: Pheres comes to see his son in 23, but in 43, it is Admetus who comes to see Clymene, in order to throw himself before her feet—a touching scene!

21. m<a>estusque beato : This telltaling antithesis reflects the proverbial truth that no wealth can buy happiness. Compare, e.g., the difference in sense between εὐδαίμων and εὐτυχής in Euripides *Medea* 1228-1230; between ὄλβιος and εὐκλεής at *Christus Patiens* 1016-1018.— *beato* | ... *toro* : Statius *Silvae* 5.1.227 f.: *beato* | ... *toro*.

22. membra toro : Verg. *Aen.* 6.220; Ovid *Pont.* 3.3.8; *Amores* 1.5.2; *Heroid.* 18.158; Silius 6.90; Statius *Theb.* 2.92 and 2.125; Juvenal 13.218: *et toto versata toro iam membra quiescunt.* Cf. Verg. *Aen.* 4.691.

toro |**et** : Our poet seems to be toying with the effect of *hiatus in caesura*—here, as well as in lines 35, 50 and 56.

atria conplet | : Ovid *Met.* 5.153: *ululatuque atria complent* |.

23. alto | **pectore** : Verg. *Aen.* 6.599 f.

24. alto | pectore suspirans : *Alcesta* 92 [= *Aen.* 2.288]: *ille autem gemitus imo de pectore ducens*; Silius 9.151 f.: *imo | pectore suspirans*: Ovid *Met.* 1.656 f.: *alto tantum suspiria ducis | pectore*; 2.655 f.: *suspirat ab imis | pectoribus*.

lacrimis <quae> causa : Verg. *Aen.* 3.305: *causam lacrimis*; Lucan 3.607: *| aeternis causam lacrimis*.

25. fatorum damna : Literally, "the harm done to his life-span," hence "his premature death". Compare Ovid *Trist.* 1.8.47 f.: *Sed quoniam accedit fatalibus hoc quoque damnis, | ut...*; Silius 4.708: *fatalia damna |*. Compare v.15.

suorum | : *C.L.E.* 965.3: *fatorum cura meorum |*. P's *sororum* is nonsensical to me, and was inspired by 4, *fatalia fila Sorores |*.

26. me rapit, ecce, dies : The reading *dies*, in the sense of "my day of death," is confirmed by 3, *da scire diem* (sc. *mortis*). P's *me rapit ecce uides* attests to the fact that the scribe sometimes attempts to alter the text of his exemplar. Compare *supra*, p. 3.

funera nato | : Ovid *Ibis* 583; Stat. *Theb.* 9.365.

27. hoc Parc<a>e docuere : The Fates reveal the imminent death of Admetus to Apollo, and Apollo—though reluctantly (28: *invitus*)— reveals it to Admetus (28: *edocuit*). There is no need to change *docuere*, since the repetition of the verb may well convey this "chain of command". Hence also *hoc Parc<a>e..., hoc noster Apollo*. And besides, we have to live with the mannerism of word-repetition when dealing with a late Latin poet: compare p. 13 f.

nefas : Cf. *C.L.E.* 1225.2 f.:

> ... annos qui vitae linquo novem atque decem.
> Heu scelus, heu crudele nefas facinusque tremendum...

noster Apollo| : Statius *Theb.* 3.627 f.: *nam te, vesane, moneri | ante nefas, unique tacet tibi noster Apollo |*. Eurip. *Bacchae* 1250: Βρόμιος ἄναξ ἀπώλεσ' οἰκεῖος γεγώς. Admetus still counts Apollo as a member of his household.

28. reddere vitam | : Ovid *Ibis* 405: *reddere vitam |*; *Trist.* 3.3.35: *reddere lucem |*; *C.L.E.* 386.6: *reddere vitam |*.

29. tu, genitor, tu... : The emotional anaphora seems to be hymnic in origin (aretalogy of a divinity). Compare Verg. *Aen.* 2.717: *| tu, genitor...*; 9.404: *| tu, dea, tu praesens nostro succurre labori*; 7.41: *| tu vatem, tu, diva, mone*.

si tempora dones : Cf. *infra*, v.73 f.; Lucan 9.534: *Aries donat sua tempora Librae |*; Seneca *Epist.* 78.17 (sc. *longus morbus*) *multum temporis donat*; Hieronym. *Epist.* 60.14.3 Hilberg: *si... Mathusalae nobis tempora donarentur...*

30. mortem subitam : Verg. *Aen.* 11.796: *subita turbatam morte Camillam* |; Lucan 9.817 f.: *subita caligine mortem* | *accipis*; Martial 6.53.3: *tam subitae mortis causam*; Seneca *Nat. Qu.* 6.28.3; Quintil. *Inst.* 7.2.14; Tac. *Ann.* 3.7.

31. concedere lucem : Claudian 28.128 f.: | *concessaque sibi...* | *luce.* Compare *concedere vitam*: *Ilias* 715 and 1037; Seneca *Medea* 185; Cicero *Ep. Fam.* 9.13.4; Livy 32.17.2.

32-42. *Pheres fails the exam in Pietas*

As we have already seen (Introduction, 6 f.), the responses of Pheres, Clymene, and Alcestis to Admetus' predicament turn around the concept of *pietas*, which seems best interpreted here as "the sense of duty of a family-member." It is a sacred duty for a member of a family to give his/her life for another member of the family. Now, neither Pheres (32), nor Clymene (45) possess this sense of family-duty. Apparently, Pheres behaves much as a *hedonist* (39 f.: <*vi*>*ta quia dulcius una* | *nil mihi*), while Clymene plays the role of a *Stoic philosopher*. Alcestis alone possesses this *pietas* (75 and 103, in addition to *pia* as referring to Alcestis in lines 78 and 99). This is her only but mighty weapon. In a marriage, this duty between the spouses is *reciprocal*. Hence Alcestis' emblem (74): *pro coniuge coniux.*

The most likely source of inspiration for our poet in the way he treats Pheres is Euripides' *Alcestis*, where Pheres' ἀψυχία is mentioned three times (642; 696; 717), and where Admetus is quite explicit (338 f.):

στυγῶν μὲν ἥ μ' ἔτικτεν, ἐχθαίρων δ' ἐμὸν
πατέρα· λόγῳ γὰρ ἦσαν, οὐκ ἔργῳ, φίλοι.

Both Pheres' arguments for rejecting Admetus' request most probably derive from Euripides (691-693 and 722; and 686-688, respectively): see Introduction, 6 f.

32. hic genitor, non ut genitor : "Hear now the father speaking unlike a father." The anaphora may reflect similar expressions in Greek tragedy, i.e., a πατὴρ ἀπάτωρ. Compare Sophocles *Electra* 1154: μήτηρ ἀμήτωρ. The idea may well come from Euripides *Alc.* 641: καί μ' οὐ νομίζω παῖδα σὸν πεφυκέναι.

si lumina poscas | : Cf. Ovid *Fasti* 2.351 f.: *inclamat comites et lumina poscit* | *Maeonis: inlatis ignibus acta patent.*

Pheres is willing to sacrifice an important part of his body—either both eyes or one hand,—but not the life itself. Now, a substitute sacrifice consisting either of a man's sight or of his right hand is puzzling. I prefer to think that the idea derives from blinding and maiming as criminal or divine punishment and retribution. The encounter with *NT* Matthew 5:29 f. (so J. K. Newman) seems a sheer coincidence to me. Compare perhaps Juvenal 13.90-94:

> Est alius metuens ne crimen *poena* sequatur;
> hic putat esse deos et peierat, atque ita secum:
> "Decernat quodcumque volet *de corpore nostro*
> Isis et irato feriat *mea lumina* sistro,
> dummodo *vel caecus* teneam quos abnego nummos..."

33. manum de corpore nostro| : Cf. Juvenal 13.92; Ovid *Heroid.* 19.84: *corpore laedatur ne manus ista meo.*

36. si qu<o>d sum : The reading is problematic. The scribe of P seems to be improvising: *sicut suum.* The strange expression, *quod sum,* should imply, *homo vivus*: "But if I grant you my entire living body [i.e., my very being], there will be nothing left of me."

37. minimam (sc. vitam) : Compare Eurip. *Alc.* 649 f. (Admetus to Pheres): βραχὺς δέ σοι | πάντως ὁ λοιπὸς ἦν βιώσιμος χρόνος.

vi tollere v<i>s iam? : "Are you after even this little life that is left to me, to snatch it away before its time?" *Iam* implies, "before its time, right away," while *vi* refers to Admetus' *insistency*: *tu, genitor, tu, sancte, potes: si tempora dones,* | *si pro me mortem subitam...* (29 f.). But the text is problematic. P seems to offer: *uis tollere u[[s]]itam.* Lebek's reading, *vis tollere, v<i>s tu,* is less likely to me because of the unconvincing repetition of *vis.* So is Parsons' reading, *vis tollere vitam?* Because of the ugly repetition, *quanta... vita... superest, minimam vis tollere vitam?*

38. | quam propter : Cf. Verg. *Aen.* 12.177: | *quam propter tantos potui perferre labores.*

mea regna : Verg. *Aen.* 2.543; *Ecl.* 1.69.

castra reliqui | : Verg. *Aen.* 10.604: *castra relinquunt* |; Lucan 2.563: *regna reliqui* |; Ovid *Met.* 13.522: *regnumque reliquit* |.

castra : i.q. *palatium,* "court," "der Hofstaat" (correctly Lebek 22). In this sense, the word is first employed by Juvenal 4.135 and *Historia Augusta* (Hadrian) 13. Later on, by Claudian 8.10; Macrobius *Sat.* 2.4.6; *C.I.L.* VI.8520; 33469; Lydus *De magistr.* 2.30.

"My kingdom and my court" seems to be an interpretation, by our poet, of the Euripidean expression, πολλῶν μὲν ἄρχεις, πολυπλέθρους δέ σοι γύας | λείψω (*Alcestis* 687 f., quoted on p. 7).

39. cont<r>istant tumul<i> : "Of the grave I dare not think." Compare Seneca *Epist.* 102.27: ... *et istuc corpus inhabitatum diu pone. Scindetur, obruetur, abolebitur: quid contristaris? Ita solet fieri...*; *De ira* 2.2.5: *Contristat nos turba maerentium.*—P has: *contustant tomul.* For the confusion of *i* and *u*, compare 78 *trustior* P, for the omission of *r*, compare: 12 *fatebo*<*r*>; 31 *digneos* (for *digne*<*r*>*is*); 82 *potneus* (for *Po*<*r*>*t*<*h*>*meus*; 91 *desere* (for *desera*<*r*>). The omission of a final vowel (like here in *tomul*) may be paralleled by 18 *car* P (for *car*<*a*>).

<*vi*>*ta quia dulcius una* | *nil mihi* : P offers *tae quam dulcior ullam nihil mihi*. I think, the reading, <*vi*>*ta*, is confirmed by Euripides *Alc.* 715 (Admetus to Pheres) : Μακροῦ βίου γὰρ ᾐσθόμην ἐρῶντά σε, as well as by *vita* in line 37 of our poem (where the scribe again writes *uitae* for *vita*). There can be little doubt that the "hedonistic" idea, attributed to Pheres by the poet, derives from Euripides. Compare particularly *Alc.* 693: τὸ δὲ ζῆν μικρόν, ἀλλ' ὅμως γλυκύ, and 722: φίλον τὸ φέγγος τοῦτο τοῦ θεοῦ, φίλον (both times Pheres speaking). I think the anaphora of φίλον in Euripides was a sufficient source of inspiration for our poet to produce the statement, <*vi*>*ta quia dulcius una* | *nil mihi*.

40. quam (sc. vitam) tu si reddere velles : The key for understanding the sense of *velles* here is the meaning of *reddere*—"to return". Evidently, Pheres is not willing to *donate* (36 *si... donavero*) the rest of his years to Admetus. But he may be willing to *lend* them to him, provided that Admetus is equally willing to *return* them (*reddere*) some day to their owner (which, Pheres is pretty sure, Admetus is unable to do). Accordingly, *velles* (if sound) would express this *ironical* connotation of, "if only you were *equally willing* to return it some day to me," implying, "if only you were able to do so."—But Hutchinson's *posses* cannot be ruled out. If it is correct, then P's *uellis* would be another improvisation on the part of the scribe, inspired by 34 *velis* (*uellis* P), or 51 *vitam concedere vellem*.

The point is, however, that Pheres closes his denial with a sarcastic sneer, devised by the poet to demonstrate a total lack of *pietas* (sense of family-duty) on the part of the father. Pretty soon, Pheres' ironical remark will be matched by a similar sarcastic argument advanced by Clymene (51 f.): "I would gladly give my life for you, if only I were sure that you could remain on earth *forever*." Both conditions belong to the class of *adynata*.

41. concessissem : This "heavy" word should be kept in the text for two reasons. First, the poet seems to be fond of this verb, since he employs it four more times (31 *tua*<*m*> *concedere lucem*; 33 *concedam*; 51 *vitam concedere vellem*; 73 *concedo*). Second, a "heavy," five-syllable word is employed also in lines 118 *corripiebat* (*diripiebat* P); 105 *soporifero*; 69 *contumulantur* (though in a *gradatio*); 71 *Pelieïa* (though an emendation and a proper name).

tumulosque <h>abitasse<m> : Cf. Petron. 71.7: *eas* (sc. *domus*), *ubi diutius nobis habitandum est*; *C.L.E.* 1267.3: *aeterna habitare domu, et saepius*.

42-70. *The long philosophical rhesis of Clymene*

As was suggested in the Introduction (7-9), Clymene's elaborate philosophical reasoning is here to counterbalance Alcestis' own *rhesis* in lines 71-103, as there can be little doubt that our poet is introducing a small *Agon* between Mother and Wife here.

Clymene comes up with no less than *five* different reasons to prove her thesis that no family-member should serve as a *vicaria victima* for another member, especially not a mother or father for her/his child. Clymene's arguments are eloquent and attest to the rhetorical skill of the Barcelona bard.

First comes a *religious* reason (46-51). It is a *crime* for a son, argues Clymene while employing the heavy word *scelerate* (47), to be the cause of destruction of his mother's *womb and breasts* (49 *uterus*; 48 *haec ubera*), the source of his own life. As is well known, womb is an old principle of life, and as such a taboo. As for Clymene's expression, *haec ubera* (48), we may even envision it as a kind of *obiectus pectorum*, on the part of the mother, thus vividly underscoring the sanctity of a mother's breasts for her son.

The second argument is more *pragmatic* (51 f.): "Why sacrificing my life for my son at all, when my death can only prolong his life on earth: it cannot bring him immortality!" The irrealis of this argument (*vitam concedere vellem,* | *si semper posses*) matches a similar sarcastic argument advanced by Pheres (40 f.: *quam tu si reddere velles,* | *nate, tibi concessissem*).

Clymene's third and main argument comes from *Stoic* philosophy. It opens with a *Senecan* statement, *Cur metui<s> mortem, cui nascimur?* (cf. Sen. *Ad Marciam* 10.5). It closes with an impressive asyndetic climax-gradatio, expressing the Heraclitean and Stoic motif of πάντα ῥεῖ—*cedunt labuntur moriuntur contumulantur* (69).

Lebek (23) has correctly referred to the rich literature *De consolatione* (notably, to R. Kassel, *Untersuchungen zur griechischen und römischen Konsolationsliteratur*, Zetemata 18, Munich, 1958, passim) as a probable source of inspiration for our poet. While Seneca remains the main source for the poet, one should not forget that, at the same time, he was an attentive reader of Euripides, where the argument, *nihil est sine morte creatum* (57), is anticipated in this form (*Alcestis* 418 f.): γίνωσκε δὲ | ὡς πᾶσιν ἡμῖν κατθανεῖν ὀφείλεται. (Cf. also 782: βροτοῖς ἅπασι κατθανεῖν ὀφείλεται).

Clymene's fourth argument is equally Stoic, while dealing with the teaching of the *inevitability* of personal fate: "My son, escape to the end of the world! And there your fate will reach you" (*<ibi> te tua fata sequentur*, 56). The same Stoic doctrine of the supreme power of Fate is reflected in Clymene's rhetorical question, *Cur ego de nato doleam, quem fata* *reposcunt?* (64), implying, Ἀνάγκῃ οὐδὲ θεοὶ μάχονται. As we have already seen (9), this argument is not valid, since the supreme Fates have already expressed their willingness to make an *exception* in the case of Admetus— *tu poteris posthac alieno vivere fato* (17).

Finally, Clymene's fifth argument (60-63 and 65-68) consists of a series of four plus five *exempla priorum* (compare 65: *sicut planxere priores*). Such catalogues of examples are an old rhetorical device, as old as Homer (compare *Iliad* 5.385-404: τλῆ μὲν Ἄρης... τλῆ δ' Ἥρη... τλῆ δ' Ἀίδης).

The former set is here to prove Clymene's thesis, "Even the gods die [i.e., go down to Hades]—temporarily, but die." Four examples follow: the famous tomb of Zeus in Crete; the dismemberment of the small boy Dionysus by the crafty Titans; and the *catabasis* of Demeter and Aphrodite. The topic of *interitus deorum* is as old as Euhemerus (Cicero *N.D.* 1.42 and 119). In addition, in Euripides *Alc.* 989 f. we read: καὶ θεῶν σκότιοι φθίνουσι / παῖδες ἐν θανάτῳ. Still, it is difficult to pinpoint the direct source of our poet. The tetrad of *exempla priorum* at Horace *Carm.* 1.28.7-11 consists of four dying heroes, not gods (Tantalus, Tithonus, Minos, Euphorbus), as does the triad at Propertius 3.18.27 f. (Nireus, Achilles, Croesus). Our poet, however, adduces four major deities (Zeus, Dionysus, Demeter, Aphrodite). Of course, the poet is cautious when speaking of the "death" of the Olympic gods: he employs such safeguards as *fertur* (60) and *fama refert* (62). His intention, however, is unmistakable: even the gods die.

Now, while the Cretan tomb of Zeus was a common knowledge in antiquity, and the *catabasis* of Demeter in search of Persephone occurs frequently enough in our sources (see *Commentary* ad lines 60 and 63), the myth of *Bacchus dissectus* (best preserved in Clement *Protr.* 17.2 and in Arnobius' translation of Clement in *Adv. nat.* 5.19), and the *catabasis* of Aphrodite to bring back Adonis (only in Aristides *Apology* 11.3) are mythological rarities, attesting to the mythological erudition of the Barcelona poet.

All four examples of the gods going down to Hades may be found in early Christian apologists: *Zeus*, in Tatian *Orat.* 27; Athenagoras *Legat.* 30; Clement *Protr.* 37.4 (Arnobius *Adv. nat.* 4.25); *Dionysus*, in Clement *Protr.* 17.2; *Demeter*, in Clement *Protr.* 17.1; *Aphrodite*, in Aristides *Apol.* 11.3. G. Harrison and D. Obbink (*ZPE* 63 [1986] 75-81) have argued for such a Christian apologetic catalogue as the most probable source for our poet. They may well be right, but there is no way of telling. For one thing, Clymene's catalogue of the noble mothers killing their own sons (65-68) does not derive from such an apologetic catalogue.

Finally, Clymene's second set of *exempla priorum* is here to prove her thesis, "Even the mothers of nobler birth than mine, even the goddesses,

have lost their sons in the past: why should I be an exception?'' Five
examples follow: Diomede lost her son Hyacinthus; Agave even tore her
son Pentheus asunder. Althaea killed Meleager, and so did the goddess
Ino with her son Melicertes. On top of that, Procne bewailed Itys, she
herself had dismembered, while collecting his bleeding entrails.

42-52. *Admetus as a criminal wretch*

43. volvitur ante pedes : Propertius 3.8.12: *haec Veneris magnae
volvitur ante pedes* |.
   vestigia... adorat | : Statius *Theb.* 12.817: *vestigia semper adora* |.
   44. inque sinus fundit lacrimas : Cf. Ovid *Fasti* 4.522: *decidit in
tepidos lucida gutta* [i.e., *lacrima*] *sinus*; *Heroid.* 6.70: *lacrimis osque sinusque
madent* |.—This is not a typical position in the hexameter for the expres-
sion, *lacrimas fundit*: compare Catull. 66.16 f.; Verg. *Aen.* 3.348; *T.L.L.*
VI.1564.42-52.
   45. | **nec pietate** : Verg. *Aen.* 1.545: | *nec pietate fuit, nec bello maior
in armis.*
   nec vincitur... fletu : Another encounter with the *Alcesta* of *A.L.*—
76 f. [= *Aen.* 4.438 f.]: *sed nullis ille* [sc. Pheres] *movetur* | *fletibus aut voces
ullas tractabilis audit.*
   46. inproperans : Rare in classical Latin (only in Petronius 38.11),
but common enough in late Latin: *Vulgate Sap.* 2:12; *Ps.* 73:10; *Pastoris
Hermae versio vulg.* 2.2 (cf. Lebek 23).
   oblitus mente parentum : Cf. Ovid *Met.* 15.451 (Lebek): *mente memor
refero. Mente,* as an *ablativus respectus* or *limitationis,* is common enough with
caecus, captus, corruptus, ictus, insanus, lapsus, motus, perversus (*T.L.L.*
VIII.720. 9-19); consequently, there is no need to read, *oblita mente.*
   47-48. |**tu, scelerate,...** |**tu tumulis gaudere meis?** The alliteration
expresses Clymene's shock and bewilderment at the nature of her son's
request. Compare a similar emotional outburst on the part of Alcestis
(72); *Me,* <*me*> *trade neci, me, coniux, trade sepulcris!* (For the alliteration
of *t* compare, e.g., *C.L.E.* 1155.6: *comprecor ut leni terra tegat tumulo.*)
   haec ubera : I think Clymene employs here the *obiectus pectorum* as a
means of imploring or imprecation. The direct source of inspiration for
our poet may well be Statius *Thebaid* 11.341 f. (Iocasta to Eteocles):

> Haec tibi canities, *haec* sunt calcanda, *nefande,*
> *ubera,* perque *uterum* sonipes hic *matris* agendus.

In case Statius' *nefande* is not sufficient to evoke the idea of (47) *scelerate,*
in our poet, there is the expression, *scelera* and *scelus,* in Statius' neighbor-
ing lines 340 and 347, respectively. Compare also Seneca *Herc. Oet.*

925 f. [Nutrix:] *Per has aniles te supplex comas | atque ubera ista paene materna obsecro*; Stat. *Theb.* 10. 694 f.: *per ego oro tuosque, | nate, meosque annos miseraeque per ubera matris...*

49. ultimus ignis : Seneca *Herc. Oet.* 1609 f.: *laetus adeone ultimos | invasit ignes?*; Quintil. *Declam.* 6.2. Cf. Seneca *Oed.* 60: *supremum ad ignem*; *Thyest.* 1090 f.: *si natos pater | humare et igni tradere extremo volo.*

50. quo te peperi : *quod te peperi* P. I prefer to keep the first person singular to match 48 *meis*; 50 *mihi*; 51 *vellem*. This creates a *hiatus in caesura*, which however may be paralleled by lines 22; 35; 56. Moreover, *uterus* as a masculine noun is much more common than is *uterum* in neuter gender. The ablative may be paralleled by Ulpian, *Dig.* 34.5.10.1: *si... haec uno utero marem et feminam peperisset...* But the alternate reading, *quod te peperi<t>*, is also possible. It would presume a *longa in arsi* (the only other example is in 85, *legat*).

51. vitam concedere vellem | : Verg. *Aen.* 11.111: *vivis concedere vellem* |.

52. ter<r>ena : The idea is, "if only I were sure you could remain on the surface of earth forever." Cf. Ausonius 3.2.24: *terrenis... in oris* |; Prudent. *Contra Symmach.* 1.590: *terrenum extendere regnum* |.

<in> sede morari | : Ovid. *Met.* 2.846: *nec in una sede morantur* | ; *Ars Amat.* 3.436: *errat et in nulla sede moratur Amor* | ; Fl. Merobaudes *De Christo* 6 Vollmer [= Claudian *Appendix* 20 (98).6]: *parvaque in sede morari* | ; Verg. *Aen.* 2.525: *et sacra longaevum in sede locavit* | ; 2.568: *secreta in sede latentem* | ; 4.504: *penetrali in sede*; Prudent. *Contra Symmach.* 1.121; 1.271: *caelesti in sede locatum* | ; *Apotheosis* (*Trin.*) 9: *dextraque in sede locare* | ; *Cathemerinon* 10.167.

53-59. *Enter Seneca: Perpetuum nihil est*

53. Cur metui<s> mortem, cui nascimur? : Seneca *Ad Marciam* (*Dial.* 6).10.5: *Si mortuum tibi filium doles, eius temporis quo natus est crimen est; mors enim illi denuntiata nascenti est; in hanc legem <erat> satus, hoc illum fatum ab utero statim prosequebatur. Epist.* 24.20: *cotidie morimur...*; Eurip. *Alc.* 418 f.: γίνωσκε δὲ | ὡς πᾶσιν ἡμῖν κατθανεῖν ὀφείλεται; 782: βροτοῖς ἅπασι κατθανεῖν ὀφείλεται.

effuge longe | : Cf. Ovid *Heroid.* 14.77: *effuge, dixi* |.

54. quo..., quo..., ubi... : "Go to the end of the world: to the extreme East, West, North or South." It is a common motif in Latin poetry: Catull. 11.2-12; Horace *Carm.* 1.22. 5-8; 2.6.1-4; Lucan 1.15-18 et alibi.

ubi barbarus ales | : *Barbarus* implies "exotic" (as does *barbaricus* in line 112), and the reference is to the miraculous bird Phoenix. Compare

Ovid *Met.* 15.392 f.: *ales:* | *Assyrii phoenica vocant*; Lucan 6.680: *cinis Eoa positi phoenicis in ara*; Pliny *N.H.* 10.3: *nobilem Arabiae phoenicem.*

55. nascitur, ac nobis iteratus fingitur orbis : "...there where the exotic bird (Phoenix) is born, so that mankind may imagine the birth of a new world-era." This is my reading and interpretation of P's: *nascitur adque nobis iteratum* [[.]]*singitur urbis.*

The scribe wrote *adque* [i.e., *atque*] for *ac*, just as he did *nihil* for *nil* in lines 36 and 40, or *ed* [i.e., *et*] *tumulusque* for *tumulosque* in line 41. A superfluous *-que* is to be found also in lines 42 and 112.—*Nobis fingitur* = *homines fingunt.*

If the suggested text is correct, the poet is clearly alluding to the *Magnus annus* linked to the rebirth of Phoenix somewhere in the Orient—either to the Egyptian Sothis cycle of 1461 solar years, or to a cycle of only 1000 or 500 years. Compare Pliny *N.H.* 10.5: *cum huius alitis* [i.e., *phoenicis*] *vita magni conversionem anni fieri*; 29.29; Claudian *Carm. min.* 27 [*Phoenix*].104 f.: *te* [sc. *phoenice*] *saecula teste* | *cuncta revolvuntur*; Herodot. 2.73; Seneca *Epist.* 42.1; Tacit. *Ann.* 6.28; Lactant. *De ave phoenice* 59-64; Clem. Rom. *Epist. ad Cor.* 25 s.f., et alibi.—For the expression, *iteratus orbis*, implying the πραγμάτων ἀποκατάστασις, compare RE XX (1914) 415 and 418, s.v. *Phoinix.*—Cf. also *supra*, p. 12 n. 7.

56. te tua fata sequentur | : Doubtless, the poet is expressing the Stoic idea of the inevitability of personal fate. Compare, e.g., Seneca's famous line (*Epist.* 107.11.5): *Ducunt volentem fata, nolentem trahunt* [cf. Hippolyt. *Refutatio* 1.21.2; *S.V.F.* I No. 527; II No. 975]. Or Horace *Carm.* 3.1.16: *omne capax movet urna nomen*; 3.1.40: *post equitem sedet atra Cura.*—*fata sequentur* | : Silius 8.38: *huc Trebiae rursum et Thrasymeni fata sequentur* | ; Propert. 2.22.19: *me licet et Thamyrae cantoris fata sequantur* |. Compare also the expression, *sequi fata*: Verg. *Aen.* 1.382: *data fata secutus* | ; 9.204: *fata extrema secutus* | ; Lucan 3.303: | *et causas, non fata, sequi*; Martial 7.44.4: *ausus es et profugi, non tua fata, sequi* |. Clymene emphasizes her point by employing (1) alliteration (*nate, late... te*); (2) anaphora (*illic...* <*ibi*>); (3) hiatus in caesura (*late:* <*ibi*>).

57. Perpetuum nihil est etc. : Seneca *Ad Polybium* (*Dial.* 11).1.1: *Ita est: nihil perpetuum, pauca diuturna sunt; aliud alio modo fragile est, rerum exitus variantur, ceterum quicquid coepit et desinit*; Manilius 1.515-517:

> Omnia mortali mutantur lege creata,
> nec se cognoscunt terrae vertentibus annis
> exutas variam faciem per saecula ferre.

Horace *Carm.* 4.7.7 f.: *immortalia ne speres, monet annus et almum* | *quae rapit hora diem*; Statius *Silvae* 2.1.218 f.: *Quicquid init ortus, finem timet. Ibimus omnes,* | *ibimus.*

58. lux rapitur : Cf. Hor. *Carm.* 4.7.8; Claudian *De Raptu Pros.* 1.96: *si rapta dies*; infra, v. 117: *lucem ra<p>tura puellae*.

moriuntur et anni : The idea is at home with the Stoics, who stress the eternity of the whole universe, not the perishability of its parts. Compare Seneca *Epist.* 24.26: *Nullius rei finis est, sed in orbem nexa sunt omnia, fugiunt ac secuntur. Diem nox premit, dies noctem, aestas in autumnum desinit, autumno hiemps instat, quae vere compescitur; omnia sic transeunt, ut revertantur*; Philo *De aeternitate mundi* 109: Καθάπερ γὰρ αἱ ἐτήσιοι ὧραι κύκλον ἀμείβουσιν ἀλλήλας ἀντιπαραδεχόμεναι πρὸς τὰς ἐνιαυτῶν οὐδέποτε ληγόντων περιόδους, τὸν αὐτὸν τρόπον καὶ τὰ στοιχεῖα τοῦ κόσμου ταῖς εἰς ἄλληλα μεταβολαῖς (τὸ παραδοξότατον) θνῄσκειν δοκοῦντα ἀθανατίζεται...

59. non<ne> : I now agree with Lebek that the sentence is interrogative (hence my supplement). The same scribal error is to be found in 8: *sit<ne>*. The sense of the line is: "Why, does not the Earth devour the very places [primarily, the mountains] she herself had previously produced?" "Verschlingt nicht die Erde die Orte, die sie zuvor hervorgebracht hatte?" (Lebek). Pliny *N.H.* 2.205 (referred to by Lebek) speaks strongly in favor of this reading: *Ipsa se comest terra: devoravit Cibotum altissimum montem cum oppido Cariae*...

Previously, I have read the line as follows: *Non est terra loco, quo <r>es generaverat ante.* "And even the (aging) Earth is no longer in the same shape in which she was when creating all these things." For *loco* [i.q. *statu, condicione*], *quo*, compare Livy 34.4.19: *Nolite eodem loco existimare, Quirites, futuram rem publicam, quo fuit antequam lex de hoc ferretur*; Verg. *Aen.* 9.723: | *et quo sit fortuna loco*; Lucan 8.558: | *quo tua sit fortuna loco*; Cato *Orat.* Fr. 2: *videsis, quo loco res publica siet*; Cic. *Legg.* 2.53; *T.L.L.* VII.1583.77-1584.52. P's *locus* (for *loco*) can be paralleled by 2 *tuus* (for *tuo*). A wrong metathesis—as in P's *se* for <r>es—is to be found in 26 *uides* (for *dies*); 52 *aeternam* (for *ter<r>ena*); 67 *ion* (for *Ino*); 90 [[de]]re'de'unt; 101 *nate* (for *ad te*); 114 *precidit* (for *percidit*).

My reasons were: (1) Such a seismic activity of Earth is not such a *self-evident truth* as to justify the rhetorical question, "Why, does not the Earth...?" (2) The verb *egenerare* cannot be documented in Latin. (3) In view of the preceding line 57, *perpetuum nihil est, nihil est sine morte creatum*, the most natural way is to take *non est*, in our line, to mean the same—"is not," instead of "does not eat."

Then, what made me change my mind? Statius, the preferred author of the Barcelona bard, in the first place. At his *Silvae* 2.1.209-211 we read:

Omnia functa
aut moritura vides: *obeunt noctesque diesque*
astraque, nec solidis prodest sua machina terris.

Combine this with 218, *Quicquid init ortus, finem timet*, with the description of a gaping chasm in the earth at *Thebaid* 7.809-817, and with Pliny *N.H.* 2.205, and you will obtain the most probable source of inspiration for our poet.

How then my objections to Lebek's reading (57) may be met? As for (1), it suffices to say that our poet is fond of rhetorical questions. They are present in lines 8; 37; 47 f.; 48-51; 53; 64 f. As for (2), the existence of the verb *egenerare* may be posited on the ground of the existence of the verb *egignere* (Lucretius 2.703: *ramos egigni corpore vivo*). Finally, (3) *ēst*, "eats," is highly recommended both by Pliny and by Statius *Theb.* 7.811: *exedit.* Compare also *Aetna* 113: *lympha perennis edit humum*; Verg. *Aen.* 5.682 f.: *lentus carinas* | *est vapor*; Stat. *Theb.* 1.508: *(exta) edet Vulcanius ignis*; *T.L.L.* V.105.42 f.—The scribal error *locus* (for *locos*) is not difficult to parallel: 41 *tumulus* (for *tumulos*); 78 *atrus* (for *atros*); 110 *pictus* (for *pictos*); 116 *arsurus* (for *arsuros*).

In their turn, the Oxonienses read the line: *non est terra loco quo se generaverat ante.* The sense is not clear enough to me. Does that mean that Earth is no longer in the same condition in which she was when she created herself? And if so, where is such a self-creation of the mother Earth to be found (certainly not at Hesiod *Theogony* 116 f.)?

60-70. *Exempla priorum: even the gods die; noble mothers mourn their dead sons*

60. pater mundi : As referring to Jupiter: *Schol. Arat.*, p. 38 Martin: βασιλεὺς δὲ τῶν ὅλων ὁ Ζεὺς καὶ πατήρ; Avienus *Arati Phaenom.* 21: | *et mundi vere sanctus* (Soubiran : *factus* A) *pater*; Seneca *Herc. Oet.* 1587: *pater rerum* (= Auson. 3.2.6; 3.6.5); Prudent. *Cathemerinon* 10. 81: *pater orbis.*

tumulatus : This clearly refers to the famous *Iovis sepulcrum* in Crete. Compare Cicero *N.D.* 3.53 [and A.S. Pease ad loc.]; Callim. *In Iovem* 8 f.; Tatian *Orat.*27; Athenag. *Leg.* 30; Clem. *Protr.* 37.4; Arnob. *Adv. nat.* 4.25; Fr. Pfister, *Der Reliquienkult im Altertum* [RGVV V.1, Giessen, 1909], 385-87; A. B. Cook, *Zeus*, I (Cambridge, 1914), 157 ff.; 645 ff.; H. Schwabl, RE Suppl. XV (1978), 1317-19 (s.v. Zeus); Harrison and Obbink, *ZPE* 63 (1986) 77 n. 13.

abisse | ... **(61) obisse** | ... **(62) perisse** | ... **(63) subisse** | : For such a chain of rhymes Lebek (24) correctly referred to *C.L.E.* 500.4-7: *meruisti* | ... *timuisti* | ... *tacuisti* | ... *obisti* |, and to *A.L.* I.1 No. 273.5-11 Riese [= 267 Shackleton Bailey]: *ligemus* | ... *metamus* | ... *secemus* | ... *perimamus* |... *crememus* |... *necemus* | ... *volemus* |. [See *Appendix.*] Add: Verg. *Aen.* 4.603-606: *fuisset* | ... *tulissem* | *implessemque...* | ... *exstinxem...* *dedissem* |.—The purpose of this rhyme-chain, consisting of four perfect infinitives, seems to be to emphasize Clymene's point: "Even the gods die—*one after the other!*" The same idea seems to be reflected in the alliteration of 63, *Cerebrum Veneremque*.

61. fratri < s > Stygii : Verg. *Aen.* 9.104; 10.113.

mutatus : Understand, *mutatus terrā*, τόπον ἀμείβων: "Jupiter changed his usual place, the surface of earth, and went down to Hades to visit his brother Pluto." Compare Ovid *Pont.* 4.14.7: *Nulla mihi cura est, terra quo muter ab ista*; *Trist.* 5.2.73 f.: *Hinc ego dum muter, vel me Zanclaea Charybdis | devoret...* It is less likely that a Zeus χθόνιος (e.g., Hesiod *Opera* 465) or καταχθόνιος (*Iliad* 9.457) should be thought of as having changed his usual Olympic outward appearance. Lebek, however, keeps P's *multatus*, "bestraft." But who is to punish a Zeus?—*Mutatus*, in the sense of "having changed his usual place," seems to be a weak "filler" here, while counterbalancing *tumulatus* of the preceding line: *tumulatus abisse* | vs. *mutatus obisse* |. Another example of a dangling *mutatus*, employed in the same sense, is provided by Prosper *De Providentia Dei* 279-282: (Lucifer) *alta | deiectus regione poli... | ... maiora nocendi | concepit verso mutatus corde venena* |, where *mutatus* implies, "after being removed from heaven."

62. Bacc < h > um... < T > ita < nu > m ex arte perisse : The myth of the small boy Dionysus, being lured by the tricky Titans with children toys and then mercilessly dismembered, is best known from Clement *Protr.* 17.2: ὃν [sc. Διόνυσον] εἰσέτι παῖδα ὄντα... δόλῳ δὲ ὑποδύντων Τιτάνων, ἀπατήσαντες παιδαριώδεσιν ἀθύρμασιν, οὗτοι δὴ οἱ Τιτᾶνες διέσπασαν, ἔτι νηπίαχον ὄντα, and from Arnobius' translation of Clement at *Adv. nat.* 5.19: *... ut occupatus puerilibus ludicris distractus ab Titanis Liber sit, ut ab isdem membratim sectus...*[1] The expression of our poem, *Titanum ex arte*, corresponds exactly to Clement's words, δόλῳ δὲ ὑποδύντων Τιτάνων. The scribe of P writes *de arte* (for *ex arte*) in the same way in which in 95 he writes *de te* (for *ex te*, maybe under the influence of 94 *de te*), and in 103 *ex me* (for *de me*).

63. vadum lethi : This is an old expression, which should be kept in the text. Compare Lucret. 5.1232: *nilo fertur minus ad vada leti* | (it little matters that the phrase is employed in a different sense here); *C.L.E.* 436.14 [*Lex perennis*] | *sisti quae cunctos iubet ad vadimonia mortis* |. Since the expression, "the stream of death," is common enough in late Latin poetry, there is no need to read, *Lethe < s >*, in spite of Seneca *Herc. Furens* 680: *placido quieta labitur Lethe vado.*—P's *uadam* (for *vadum*) may be paralleled by 44 *lacrimum* P (for *lacrimas*), or 103 *exempla* (for *exemplum*). As for P's *lechi* (for *lethi*), compare 2 [[*t*]]çectas; 9 ṭamen (or çamen) P.

---

[1] Also 1.41; Aristid. *Apol.* 10.8; Justin 1 *Apol.* 21.2; Orig. *c. Cels.* 3.23; *Acta Apollonii* 22; Ps.-Nonnus Abbas [VI], *Histor. Gregorii in Iulianum*: ad Greg. *Orat.* II *c. Iul.* 35 (*P. G.* 36, 1053 C).

Cererem : For the *catabasis* of Demeter in search of Persephone, compare: Verg. *Georg.* 1.39; Hygin. *Fab.* 251; Orphic Hymn 41.5; Olympiodorus *In Plat. Phaedon.* I, p. 115 Westerink; Schol. Pind *Ol.* 6.160a; *Suda*, s.v. βάραθρον [= Schol. Aristoph. *Plut.* 431], and Harrison and Obbink, *o.c.*, 76 f.—Most probably Clement too knew of the *catabasis* of Demeter at *Protreptic* 17.1: ... καὶ τὸ σχίσμα τῆς γῆς καὶ τὰς ὗς τὰς Εὐβουλέως τὰς συγκαταποθείσας ταῖν θεαῖν [i.e., Demeter and Persephone], δι᾽ ἣν αἰτίαν ἐν τοῖς Θεσμοφορίοις μεγαρίζοντες χοίρους ἐμβάλλουσιν. In his very summary report, Clement assumes that Demeter entered Hades through *the same chasm* through which Persephone previously had been carried down by Pluto. Consequently, there is no need to change ταῖν θεαῖν into τοῖν θεοῖν, as Wilamowitz did. Evidently, Clement shares his source with Schol. Lucian p. 275.25 ff. Rabe, where we read: ... Εὐβουλεύς τις συβώτης ἔνεμεν ὗς καὶ συγκατεπόθησαν τῷ χάσματι τῆς Κόρης· εἰς οὖν τιμὴν τοῦ Εὐβουλέως ῥιπτεῖσθαι τοὺς χοίρους εἰς τὰ χάσματα τῆς Δήμητρος καὶ τῆς Κόρης. Compare, e.g., Fritz Graf, *Eleusis und die orphische Dichtung Athens in vorhellenistischer Zeit* [RGVV XXXIII, Berlin, 1974], 165 n. 36.

Veneremque : The *catabasis* of Aphrodite to bring back Adonis is preserved only in Aristides *Apology* 11.3 [leaving apart the references posterior to the time of our poet, roughly A.D. 350: see *Appendix*]:[1] Ἀφροδίτην λέγουσιν καὶ εἰς Ἅιδου καταβῆναι, ὅπως ἀγοράσῃ τὸν Ἄδωνιν ἀπὸ τῆς Περσεφόνης. Contrast Hyginus *Fab.* 251: *Qui licentia Parcarum ab inferis redierunt*: 4. *Adonis... voluntate Veneris.*

Again, the fact that all four major gods who go down to Hades appear in Christian apologetic writers (Aristides, Tatian, Athenagoras, Clement) may be of significance while indicating that such a Christian catalogue of "dying gods" served as the source for our poet (so Harrison and Obbink). One should not forget, however, that our *poeta doctus* often prefers to combine several sources in one single line; that the catalogue of heroines (65-68) does not derive from any Christian catalogue; finally, that already in Euripides' *Alcestis* 989 f. we read: καὶ θεῶν σκότιοι φθίνουσι / παῖδες ἐν θανάτῳ. My point is that we are dealing with a sophisticated, learned, and eclectic poet, who combines his sources in a rather centonic procedure.

64. | **Cur ego... doleam?** ... (65) | **Cur ego non plangam?** : An old rhetorical device: Cicero *Catil.* 4.2: *Cur ego non laeter?* *Pis.* 79: *Cur ego non ignoscam?*; Ovid Fr. 6: *Cur ego non dicam, Furia, te furiam?*; *Amores* 2.11.54: *Cur ego non votis blandiar ipse meis?*; Persius 5.89: *Cur mihi non liceat...?*;

---

[1] They are: Cyrill. Alex. *In Is.* II.3 (*P.G.* 70, 441 AB); Procop. Gaz. *In Is.* 18 (*P.G.* 87, 2137 f.); Ps.-Nonnus 38 ed. J. Declerk, *L'Antiquité Classique* 45 (1976) 184 f.

Statius *Achill.* 1.949 f.: *cur non ego Martia tecum | signa feram?*; Martial 3.99.3 f.: *Cur ludere nobis | non liceat...?*, et saepius.

quem fata reposcunt | : Propert. 2.1.71: *quandocumque igitur vitam mea fata reposcent*; Ovid *Met.* 13.180: *arma peto: vivo dederam, post fata reposco.* Compare *Alcesta* 82 f.: *| stat sua cuique dies* [= *Aen.* 10.467]... *| utere sorte tua* [= *Aen.* 12.932]: *patet atri ianua Ditis* [= *Aen.* 6.127].

66. Diomede : The name of Hyacinthus' mother is a mythological rarity. Incidentally, take notice of the liberty with which the scribe of P converts *heroines* into *heroes*: *Diomede* into *Diomedes*, *Agaue* into *Acatem* (i.e., *Achatem*), *Ino* into *Ion* (67).

67. dea perdidit Ino : Ino (Leucothea), driven mad by Hera, throws herself into the sea with her infant son Melicertes in her arms. Apparently, our poet follows the story as found in Ovid's *Met.* 4.527-530: *... Ino, | seque super pontum nullo tardata timore | mittit onusque suum* [i.e., Melicertes, cf. v. 522]. (Just as in our line 66, Ino is linked with Agaue in Ovid as well: *Met.* 4.429-431.) In his *Medea* (1282-1289), however, Euripides makes Ino kill both her sons (Learchus and Melicertes), probably in order to bring Ino closer to the case of Medea.—The force of the epithet *dea* may be in Clymene's point, "if a *goddess* could kill her own son, why should not I, a mortal woman, be allowed to lose my son?"

68. flevit Ityn Progne : Compare Horace *Carm.* 4.12.5 f.: *Ityn flebiliter gemens, | infelix avis...*; Martial 10.51.4: *Ismarium paelex Attica plorat Ityn*; Ovid *Amores* 3.12.32: *concinit Odrysium Cecropis ales Ityn.*

colligit ilia cruda | : Compare *exta... cruda* in Ovid *Fasti* 6.518; Martial 11.57.4; Livy 29.27.5; *vulnera cruda* in Ovid *Pont.* 1.3.16; Juvenal 2.73; Pliny *Epist.* 5.16.11.—This is the preferred position for the word *ilia*, cf. Ovid *Ibis* 169 f.:

> Unguibus et rostro *crudus* trahet *ilia* vultur
> et scindent avidi perfida corda canes.

Statius *Silvae* 5.2.115 f.: *vexantemque ilia nuda | calce ferocis equi*; Silius 13.594. It does not seem difficult to imagine that either Statius' *ilia nuda* or Ovid's *crudus... ilia vultur* could have evoked in our poet *ilia cruda*.

P offers, however: *colligit illa cruentus* [voluit: *cruentum*]. This I take to be a makeshift, on the part of our scribe, after the loss of the last syllable of the line. For *illa* (i.e., Procne) is redundant, and *cruentum*, "covered with blood," is simply unconvincing when dealing with the *dismembered body* of Itys. Finally, the verb *colligit*, "she gathers together, collects," speaks in favor of *ilia* = *viscera*, "intestines, entrails," not *illa*. As for *illa* (for *ilia*), compare 6 *luit* P (for *iuit*). As for *cruentus* (for *cruda*), compare similar line-end makeshifts in 8 *uitam* P (for *regna*); 25 *sororum* P (for *suorum*); 37 *uitam* (?) P (for *vis iam*); 39 *ullam* P (for *una*); 66 *acatem* P (for *Agaue*); 67 *ion* P (for *Ino*). Compare *Index*, p. 111.

70. tegit < ca > eli v < i > s : This is Lebek's convincing restoration of P's *legit illius*, with the help of Ovid *Met.* 1.26: *vis... caeli*. (1) *legit* for *tegit*: compare the reverse error (*t* for *l*) in 2 *laurus... tectas* P (for *lectas*) and in 85 *vestigia ne mea... tegat* (for *legat*). (2) After *-it* of *legit*, the letter *c* of *celi* was dropped because of the similarity between *t* and *c* (compare 63 *lechi* P, for *lethi*). (3) *illi* is a corruption of < *c* > *eli*: our scribe writes *i* for *e* also in lines 48 *ubira* (for *ubera*); 40 *uellis* (for *velles*); 52 *possis* (for *posses*); 87 *digna retinere* (for *dignare tenere*); 104 *alis* (for *ales*). (4) Finally, *us* stands for *v* < *i* > *s*: compare 37 *v* < *i* > *s*; 39 *tumul* < *i* >.

In conclusion, *caeli vis* is the correct reading here, and it is a sure Ovidian echo. *Met.* 1.26-29 reads as follows:

> Ignea convexi *vis* et sine pondere *caeli*
> emicuit summaque locum sibi fecit in arce.
> Proximus est *aër* illi *levitate* locoque;
> densior his *tellus...*

Now, the point is that both Lebek's translation ("was die Kraft des Himmels... bedeckt"), and my own previous translation ("whatever lives under the heavenly vault") are not exact. For doubtless, Ovid's expression, *ignea... vis... caeli*, refers to the Stoic *fiery ether*. Compare *Met.* 1.81: *aethere*; 15.243: *aër atque aëre purior ignis*; *S.V.F.* I No. 116: Ζήνων πύρινον εἶναι τὸν οὐρανόν, and Franz Bömer ad *Met.* 1.26. Take notice that both Ovid and our poet combine *ether* with *air*. Consequently, the clause means, "whatever is encompassed by the heavenly ether and the roaming air," while implying, "all living beings *on earth*." For, according to the Stoic doctrine followed by Ovid, the earth is the world-mass which is being encompassed by ether and air.

There is no need for introducing "earth" and "sea" into the text—as the Oxonienses do while reading the line: *nam quaecumque gerit tellus < mare > vel vagus aër*. Leaving apart the fact that *legit illius* is not a likely scribal error of *gerit tellus*, the point is that the Stoic expression, "whatever is covered by ether and air," refers to all living creatures *both* on earth and in the sea. For the Stoics considered sea as *part* of the earth: Κόσμος μὲν οὖν ἐστι σύστημα ἐξ οὐρανοῦ καὶ γῆς καὶ τῶν ἐν τούτοις περιεχομένων φύσεων (Chrysippus ap. Arium Didymum Fr. 31 Diels; Posidonius ap. Diog. Laert. 7.138; Ps.-Aristotle *De mundo* 2, p. 391 b 9).

vagus aër : Tibull. 3.7.21; cf. Catull. 65.17; Ovid *Met.* 8.197: *vaga... aura* |; 1.75: *agitabilis aër* |; *T.L.L.* 1.1051.25-61.

69. As a rule, the catalogue of *exempla priorum* should not form the end of a *rhesis*, which is reserved for, say, a *peroratio*. Accordingly, in her closing lines (70-69) Clymene returns to her main argument—(53) *Cur metui <s> mortem, cui nascimur?*, and (57) *Perpetuum nihil est*. In a kind of *Ringcomposition*, she then produces a pointed conclusion (in 70-69) about the absolute necessity of death for all living beings on earth: *cedunt labuntur moriuntur contumulantur*. The form of her expression is an elegant climax-*gradatio* (four asyndetic atemporal presents, consisting of 2 + 3 + 4 + 5 syllables). The isoteleuta successfully convey the idea of the inevitability of death. Parsons' transposition of lines 69 and 70, and Dihle's transposition of words in 70 are absolutely necessary.

contumulantur : "and are buried for good." Compare Ovid *Trist.* 3.3.32; *Ibis* 462; Martial 8.57.4; Apul. *Met.* 1.13.

71-103. *Alcestis' rhesis: exemplum pietatis*

Clymene's and Alcestis' *rhesis* consist of three "blocks" each (Clymene's performance covers some 29 lines, while Alcestis' plea takes 33 lines, assuming that the lacuna between lines 101 and 102 is no longer than one line only). But what a difference in content between the two women! While the Mother employs a heavy artillery of philosophical and mythological arguments, the Wife relies on a moral one—on the sense of duty of a family-member (φίλος), which she calls her *pietas* (75; 103; *pia*: 78; 99).

As we have already seen (*Introduction*, 9 f.), Alcestis' *anti-rhesis* may be divided into two parts. In its first part (71-82), she tries to demonstrate her thesis about the *pietas* between the members of a family. In the second part (83-103), she takes care of two different things: (1) she entreats her husband not to forget her after her self-denying death; (2) to take good care of her small orphans.

Now, Alcestis' eloquence was crucial for the success of this *ethopoeia*. That is why the Barcelona bard, in depicting the *ethos* and the *pathos* of his heroine, heavily borrows both ideas and diction from Euripides, Vergil, Horace, Propertius (both Cornelia and Cynthia), Ovid, Silius, Statius, and the sepulchral poetry (*C.L.E.*) as well.

In her *Certamen* with Clymene, Alcestis offers three counter-arguments to prove her thesis. One of them (about *pietas*) would have done. But the rules of an *Agon* dictate that no *rhesis* may consist of one single rhetorical argument. Alcestis' first reason is that, after her heroic death, immense glory will be in store for her: *laus magna mei post funera nostra* (76), since her noble feat will be remembered through centuries and generations to come. Most probably, this argument derives from the traditional myth (cf. Eurip. *Alc.* 623 f.; *Alcesta* 154).

Her second argument, however, is an obvious rhetorical improvisation, on the part of our poet. Alcestis claims, by sacrificing her life for her husband, she would be spared a *widow's wretched life* of everlasting mourning and sorrow—*lacrimosa recedat | vita procul: mors ista placet* (80 f.).

Her third and main argument, on which her *laus magna* depends, is her *pietas*, her sense of family duty, loyalty and commitment (75 f.):

> Si vinco matrem, vinco *pietate* parentem,
> *si m < or > ior*, laus magna mei post funera nostra.

It is a sacred duty for *every* member of a family (small children being not excluded: remember Apollo's words of 19, *natique rudes*) to offer his/her life for another member of the same family, in case of necessity. Alcestis' point, however, is that *the spouses* have a special obligation in fulfilling this sacred law, and that in a marriage such a duty is *reciprocal*. Now, this particular duty of a spouse to give her/his life for her/his partner is expressed in the final injunction of Alcestis addressed to her husband (102 f.): *Et tu pro coniuge cara | disce mori...!* ("You too, Admetus, learn to give your life for your (future) dear wife (if need be)...!"). As for the reciprocity of this duty between the spouses, it is eloquently expressed in the Ovidian clausula, *pro coniuge coniux |* (74), which Alcestis adopts for her own slogan.

What served as a source of inspiration for our poet in presenting his heroine as an *exemplum pietatis* (103)? As we have already mentioned (10), the possibility that the myth of the killing of Pelias by his daughters was such a source for our poet cannot be ruled out. There Alcestis appears as possessing a *special and inborn* sense of *pietas*-εὐσέβεια, even before marrying Admetus. The report of Diodorus is instructive. While the rest of Pelias' daughters (four of them: Pelopia, Medusa, Pisidice, Hippothoe) did engage in killing their father, Alcestis, the oldest daughter, refused to take part in this heinous crime—δι' εὐσεβείας ὑπερβολήν. (Compare Diodorus 4.52.2: Καὶ τὰς μὲν ἄλλας ἁπάσας [sc. παρθένους] τὸν πατέρα τυπτούσας ἀποκτεῖναι, μόνην δ' Ἄλκηστιν δι' εὐσεβείας ὑπερβολὴν ἀποσχέσθαι τοῦ γεννήσαντος.) It is as a reward for her *pietas* that Alcestis was given in marriage to Admetus: Φασὶ δ' Ἄλκηστιν τὴν Πελίου θυγατέρα, μόνην τῆς κατὰ τὸν πατέρα ἀσεβείας οὐ μετασχοῦσαν, δοθῆναι γυναῖκα δι' εὐσέβειαν Ἀδμήτῳ (Diodor. 6.8.1).

One may, however, ask: What proof do we have that the Barcelona bard knew the myth of the killing of Pelias? On the other hand, we have sufficient proof that our poet was a very attentive reader of Euripides' *Alcestis*. Consequently, it seems methodologically preferable to look for the source of Alcestis' *pietas* in Euripides alone. I feel that the idea of *pietas*, understood as a sense of duty between the relatives (φίλοι) within a family, is sufficiently present in the play to serve as a source for our poet. Compare particularly *Alcestis* 15-18; 338 f.; 641-647:

15   Πάντας δ' ἐλέγξας καὶ διεξελθὼν φίλους,
      πατέρα γεραιόν θ' ἥ σφ' ἔτικτε μητέρα,
      οὐχ ηὗρε πλὴν γυναικὸς ὅστις ἤθελε
      θανὼν πρὸ κείνου μηκέτ' εἰσορᾶν φάος.

338   στυγῶν μὲν ἥ μ' ἔτικτεν, ἐχθαίρων δ' ἐμὸν
      πατέρα· λόγῳ γὰρ ἦσαν, οὐκ ἔργῳ, φίλοι.

641   καί μ' οὐ νομίζω παῖδα σὸν πεφυκέναι.
      ἦ τἄρα πάντων διαπρέπεις ἀψυχίᾳ,
      ὃς τηλικόσδ' ὢν κἀπὶ τέρμ' ἥκων βίου
      οὐκ ἠθέλησας οὐδ' ἐτόλμησας θανεῖν
      τοῦ σοῦ πρὸ παιδός, ἀλλὰ τήνδ' εἰάσατε
      γυναῖχ' ὀθνείαν, ἣν ἐγὼ καὶ μητέρα
      πατέρα τέ γ' ἐνδίκως ἂν ἡγοίμην μόνην.

So much Apollo and Admetus about the duty of a relative (φίλος). Alcestis is even more explicit (180-182):

      προδοῦναι γάρ σ' ὀκνοῦσα καὶ πόσιν
   θνῄσκω. σὲ δ' ἄλλη τις γυνὴ κεκτήσεται,
   σώφρων μὲν οὐκ ἂν μᾶλλον, εὐτυχὴς δ' ἴσως.

(Alcestis to her marriage bed: "I die because I hated to *betray* you and my husband. Now, another wife will obtain you. More fortunate than I? Perhaps. *Wiser* than I? Never."). Alcestis' σωφροσύνη is best explained as her ethical and religious wisdom. And this wisdom finds its manifestation in the readiness, on the part of the heroine, to sacrifice her life for her husband while fulfilling her duty deriving from their marital bond (*pietas*).

Plato seems to follow Euripides in his treatment of the σωφροσύνη-*pietas* of Alcestis, based on the duty between the relatives of a family (φίλοι). For at *Symposion* 179 c 1, he states that Alcestis had surpassed both parents of Admetus in the bond of family love and commitment— ὑπερεβάλετο τῇ φιλίᾳ. This statement seems to echo Euripides' line 339, λόγῳ γὰρ ἦσαν, οὐκ ἔργῳ, φίλοι (sc. Admetus' parents).

My conclusion is that the concepts of φιλία and σωφροσύνη in Euripides' *Alcestis* are the main source of the idea of *pietas*, in our poet, where *coniux pia* (78) may well echo γυνὴ σώφρων of Euripides' *Alcestis* 182.

83-92. *Alcestis and Laodamia, Cynthia and Cornelia*

While the first "block" or passage of Alcestis' *rhesis* (71-82) pretty much follows Euripides in the ideas of *pietas* (75), *pro coniuge coniux* (74), and *laus magna mei post funera nostra* (76), its second "block" (83-92) considerably departs from the traditional myth. For in these short ten lines, the imagination of the Barcelona bard has managed to combine elements deriving from Euripides' Alcestis, Ovid's Laodamia, and Propertius' Cynthia and Cornelia, as I shall try to demonstrate.

As has been already mentioned (10 f.), the most striking contrast between the traditional myth and our poem is in the fact that our Alcestis does take into consideration the possibility of a *second wife* for Admetus. The Euripidean Alcestis emphatically demands that Admetus promise never to marry again. The fear of an *evil stepmother* for her small orphans, which is usually "as kind as a viper" (310), serves as the main reason for the heroine to beg her husband never to remarry (*Alcestis* 305-310; 372 f.):

305   ... καὶ μὴ 'πιγήμῃς τοῖσδε μητρυιὰν τέκνοις,
        ἥτις κακίων οὖσ' ἐμοῦ γυνὴ φθόνῳ
        τοῖς σοῖσι κἀμοῖς παισὶ χεῖρα προσβαλεῖ.
        μὴ δῆτα δράσῃς ταῦτά γ', αἰτοῦμαί σ' ἐγώ.
        ἐχθρὰ γὰρ ἡ 'πιοῦσα μητρυιὰ τέκνοις
310   τοῖς πρόσθ', ἐχίδνης οὐδὲν ἠπιωτέρα.
372   ... μὴ γαμεῖν ἄλλην ποτὲ
        γυναῖχ' ἐφ' ὑμῖν [sc. παισὶ] μηδ' ἀτιμάσειν ἐμέ.

In his part, Admetus gladly gives this promise (328-331 and 374), while their children serve as witnesses to his binding words (371-373).

In addition, the *Alcesta* of the *Latin Anthology* follows Euripides (125-128):
"O dulcis coniux [*Aen.* 2.777], *castum servare cubile* [8.412]
sis memor [12.439]; extremum hoc munus morientis habeto [*Ecl.* 8.60],
si bene quid de te merui [*Aen.* 4.317], *lectumque iugalem* [4.496]
natis parce tuis [10.532]. Sic, sic iuvat ire sub umbras [4.660]."

Our Alcestis, however, is entertaining the possibility of a second wife for her husband. For, first of all, there is the force of the *comparatives* in lines 84-85:

        Hoc tantum moritura rogo, ne post mea fata
        dulcior ulla tibi, vestigia ne mea *coniux*
85   *carior* ista legat. Et tu...

("Before I die, I have only one wish for you. After I am gone, may you never love another woman *as much as you did me*; may the wife to take my place never be *dearer to your heart than I have been*! As for you..."). Now, if the comparatives, *dulcior ulla*, and, *coniux carior*, have any force at all, then it is only natural to conclude that Alcestis is envisioning here the possibility of a second wife for Admetus. This idea seems to be even a probability and a necessity for a young widower with small children.

If my interpretation of the text is correct, Alcestis has nothing against a second marriage of Admetus, provided that she remain his *first and greatest love* (*ne... dulcior ulla tibi*). If so, then the expression of 84 f., *vestigia ne mea coniux* | *carior ista legat*, implies that Admetus' future wife— naturally enough—would take Alcestis' place in his *household*, but not in his heart as well. In other words, his second marriage should be a marriage of convenience, not of love.

In spite of some exaggerations on the part of our poet, Alcestis' point seems to be clear enough. She takes every precaution not to be completely forgotten by her husband after her self-denying death for him. Take notice of the force of the correspondence between the expressions, *ne desera<r> a te* |, and, *quod vitam desero pro te* |, in lines 91-92 (both expressions being placed in a strategically visible position in a line):

Qualiscumque tamen, coniux, ne desera<r> a te,
nec doleam de me, quod vitam desero pro te.

Or the force of *paulum* in line 101: "But if you neglect me, if the sweet image of me does not come to your mind *from time to time...*".

Secondly, there is the presence of a *stepmother* for Alcestis' small orphans in lines 98-99. This presence is so vivid and elaborate that it must make part of a real possibility. For if our Alcestis did not allow her husband to remarry, then why mention the remote possibility of an avenging dead mother at all (*matris pia vindicet umbra*)?

Finally, there is the expression, *coniux cara*, in lines 102-103: *Et tu pro coniuge cara* | *disce mori...* ("And you too, Admetus, learn to die for your (new) dear wife...!"). However, P has *caro*, not *cara*. If our poet had really written, *pro coniuge caro*, not, *pro coniuge cara*, then Alcestis is no longer addressing her husband here, since both, *Et tu*, and, *pro coniuge caro*, cannot refer to the same person (Admetus).

Lebek (27) alternately keeps *caro* in the text ("für den lieben Gatten"), while understanding the allocution, *Et tu*, of line 102, as a kind of *parabasis*. According to him, Alcestis is addressing here *a future young female reader* of the poem: "Alcestis würde sich dann abschliessend an die Leserin oder Hörerin wenden und sie auffordern, ihrem Beispiel zu folgen." In my view, such an intruding *parabasis* is highly unlikely, since it would destroy the thematic unity of the eloquent *rhesis* of Alcestis, which is being addressed to her husband in the first place.

My reasons for the change of *caro* into *cara* are as follows. First, Alcestis' long *rhesis*, addressed to Admetus, badly needs a *final moral injunction* in her closing lines, also addressed to Admetus. Such a final

instruction for her husband is provided by the pathetic advocacy for
pietas, comprised in lines 102-103: "*Learn* to die for your (future) dear
wife, *learn* from my example what a sense of *duty* (*pietas*) is!" It is not difficult to understand why Alcestis feels that her husband badly needs such
a final moral instruction for his *future life*, since throughout the poem he
appears as dejected and afraid of death. For one thing, his "endless crying" strikes the eyes (in lines 22; 24; 44; 45; 71).

Second, the allocution of line 85, *Et tu* [sc. *Admete*], makes it likely that
the allocution of line 102, *Et tu*, also refers to Admetus. There, *Et tu* was
opposed to *coniux carior*, "your future wife." Here, *Et tu* is most probably
opposed to *ego*, hiding in the lacuna of the same line.

Finally, an extremely illiterate and careless scribe who was able of
writing, e.g., 18 *genetrix... car* (for *genetrix... car<a>*); 76 *nostro* (for
nostra); 63 *uadam* (for *vadum*); 103 *exempla* (*exemplum*), is equally capable
of writing *caro* for *cara* in 102. In conclusion, we are dealing here with an
easy emendation of a last letter in a line.

Consequently, if Alcestis' consideration of a second wife for Admetus
is a probability, one may ask: Why did our poet change the traditional
myth? To be sure, already the Euripidean Alcestis does not rule out completely the possibility of a second marriage for Admetus. For when bidding farewell to her marriage bed, she says (181): θνῄσκω. σὲ δ' ἄλλη τις
γυνὴ κεκτήσεται, "I die. Now, *another wife* will obtain you." Either
Alcestis had changed her mind between her lines 181 and 305, or there
is a difference between what she demands from her husband and what
she thinks and says *when alone*, or else Euripides is inconsistent here, I do
not know. My point is that the idea of a second wife for the widower
comes to Alcestis' mind, and that Euripides remains a possible source for
our poet.

The main reason, however, for the introduction of a possible second
wife for Admetus is, in my opinion, the influence of the *regina elegiarum*
upon our poet. Propertius needed the prospect of a second wife for
Paullus in order to introduce and then exploit the touching motif of a
noverca for Cornelia's small orphans—to leave apart here the expectancy
of a second marriage for a young widower with small children in contem-
porary Roman society (Prop. 4.11.85-90):

85   Seu tamen adversum mutarit ianua lectum,
          sederit et nostro cauta *noverca* toro,
      coniugium, pueri, laudate et ferte paternum:
          capta dabit vestris moribus illa manus;
      nec matrem laudate nimis: collata priori
90   vertet in offensas libera verba suas.

The same reason will hold for our poet as well: he exploits the *noverca-motif* in his lines 98-99:

> Quos, rogo, ne parvos man < u > s indigna < nda > *novercae*
> prodat, et < h > eu flentes matris pia vindicet umbra.

Now, there can be no doubt that the Barcelona poet knew the Cornelia elegy well. Compare his lines 93, *Ante omnes commendo tibi pia pignora natos*, and 99, with Prop. 4.11.73 f.:

> Nunc tibi commendo communia pignora natos:
> haec cura et cineri spirat inusta meo.

Another borrowing from the *regina elegiarum* may hide in his line 94, *pignora, quae solo de te fecunda creavi*, echoing Cornelia's words, *uni nupta*, and, *fac teneas unum nos imitata virum* (4.11.36 and 68).

In addition, both Propertius and the Barcelona bard borrow ideas from Euripides. As for the former, compare Cornelia's words, *fungere maternis vicibus, pater* (4.11.75), with Eurip. *Alcestis* 377, σὺ νῦν γενοῦ τοῖσδ᾽ ἀντ᾽ ἐμοῦ μήτηρ τέκνοις, and Prop. 4.11.82 f.:

> somniaque [sc. Paulli] in faciem credita saepe
> meam [sc. Corneliae]:
> atque ubi secreto nostra ad simulacra loqueris...

with Eurip. *Alc.* 348-352 and 354-356 (quoted below, p. 70 f.). [H. E. Butler and E. A. Barber, *The Elegies of Propertius*, Oxford, 1933, p. 385, mention two out of the three coincidences with Euripides.] As for the latter, his expression, *man < u > s indigna < nda > novercae* (98), seems to be a direct borrowing from Euripides' line 307, τοῖς σοῖσι κἀμοῖς παισὶ χεῖρα προσβαλεῖ [sc. μητρυιά].

However, while the idea, *matris pia... umbra* (99), may be present in Cornelia's words, *haec cura et cineri spirat inusta meo* (Prop. 4.11.74), on the other hand, the ideas of *flentes*, on the part of Alcestis' orphans, and *vindicet*, on the part of the caring deceased mother (99), are absent both in Euripides and Propertius. Consequently, I think that our poet is combining here Cornelia's words with the extremely popular *folkloric motif* of the dead mother *avenging* her mistreated orphans *even from her grave*: Compare Stith Thompson, E221.2.1; E323.2; H. Bächtold-Stäubli, *Handwörterbuch des deutschen Aberglaubens*, VI (1934-35), 697; J. Bolte and G. Polívka, *Anmerkungen zu den Kinder- und Hausmärchen der Brüder Grimm*, I (Leipzig, 1913; reprint Hildesheim, 1963), p. 96 (ad Grimm, Nos. 11 and 13). This may serve as another illustration of the sophistication of the Barcelona bard.

The effigy (**87**) *and the ghost* (**90**) *of Alcestis*

The next problem in the new poem is even more intriguing. While entreating her husband to keep loving her after her death, our Alcestis says: "As for you, keep loving me! I mean it, not in name only! *Think that you are sleeping with me during the night!* Do not hesitate to take *my ashes* into your lap, to caress them with a firm hand!" (85-88). "If it is true that *shades* return, *I shall come* to lie down with you. Whatever shape I may have then, my husband, abandon me not!" (90-91).

Alcestis' demand (85-88) and her promise (90) contain two different motifs—Alcestis' *"ashes"* (87, *cineres*), and her *"shade"* (90, *umbra*). Now, while the former motif may be explained by means of Euripides' *Alcestis* 348-352, the latter one can not.

Let us take Alcestis' request concerning her *cineres* first (85-88):

> Et tu, ne<c> nomine tantum,
> me cole, meque puta tecum sub nocte iacere.
> *In gremio cineres nostros dignare tenere,*
> *nec timida tractare manu...*

Probably imitating the example of Laodamia (compare Euripides' *Protesilaus*; Hygin. *Fab.* 104; Apollodor. *Epitome* 3.30; Eustath. ad *Iliad.* 2.701 [I, p. 507.3 van der Valk], et alibi), the Euripidean Admetus promises Alcestis that, after her death, he will order the best sculptors to make an image of her to be placed in their bedchamber. Now, presumably during the night and being alone, Admetus would then embrace and caress the effigy of his beloved dead wife, and even talk to it:

> 348   Σοφῇ δὲ χειρὶ τεκτόνων δέμας τὸ σὸν
>   εἰκασθὲν ἐν λέκτροισιν ἐκταθήσεται,
> 350   ᾧ προσπεσοῦμαι καὶ περιπτύσσων χέρας
>   ὄνομα καλῶν σὸν τὴν φίλην ἐν ἀγκάλαις
>   δόξω γυναῖκα καίπερ οὐκ ἔχων ἔχειν.

The same Laodamia motif is present in Propertius' Cornelia elegy (*atque ubi secreto nostra ad simulacra loqueris...*, 4.11.83), and, of course, in the Laodamia story in Ovid's *Heroides* 13.151-158:

> Dum tamen arma geres diverso miles in orbe,
>   quae referat vultus est mihi *cera* tuos:
> illi blanditias, illi tibi debita verba
>   dicimus, *amplexus accipit illa meos.*
> 155   Crede mihi, plus est, quam quod videatur, imago:
>   adde sonum cerae, Protesilaus erit.

Hanc specto teneoque sinu pro coniuge vero
et, tamquam possit verba referre, queror.

Euripides is the most probable source of inspiration for our poet as well. For Alcestis' expression of line 87, *cineres nostros*, cannot refer to the *urn with her ashes*, which is referred to by the word, *favillae* (88). As is normal, after the cremation of the heroine (116: *arsurosque omnes secum...*), her bones will be buried in a tomb of the cemetery, and her ashes will be kept in an urn to be placed either in a niche or in a vault on her grave. This is being referred to by the words of our poem, *favillae* (88), and *titulus*, "tombstone" (89), respectively.

Consequently, the word *cineres* (87) has the *metaphorical* sense of "ashes as the condition of the body after death (whether cremated or not)" (*Oxford Latin Dictionary*, s.v., 4a). Compare, e.g., Statius *Theb.* 8.113: *nec attonito saltem cinis ibo parenti*. In other words, *cineres* means here, "ashes as a shadow," or rather, "ashes as an *image* of the deceased person."

Now, in view of the fact that the statue of Alcestis in Euripides (and probably also the statue of Cornelia in Propertius) is a full-size one (*Alc.* 350: ᾧ προσπεσοῦμαι), while the effigy of Alcestis in our poem is a smaller one, if it is to be taken into Admetus' *lap*, just as seems to be Protesilaus' effigy in the lap of Laodamia, I think the probability is that the Barcelona poet combines here Euripides with Ovid, *Heroid.* 13.157: *Hanc* [sc. *ceram Protesilai*] *specto teneoque sinu pro coniuge vero.*

The latter motif, that of Alectis' *umbra* or "shade," is even more difficult to assess. For while the Euripidean deceased Alcestis may come to visit her husband *in his dreams alone*:

354   Ἐν δ' ὀνείρασι
φοιτῶσά μ' εὐφραίνοις ἄν· ἡδὺ γὰρ φίλους
κἂν νυκτὶ λεύσσειν, ὅντιν' ἂν παρῇ χρόνον

—just as Cornelia would do with Paullus: *somniaque in faciem credita saepe meam* (4.11.82),—the shade of our Alcestis would do much more than that. During the night, she would come to Admetus' bedchamber *to lie down with him* (90):

Si redeunt umbr<a>e, veniam tecum<que> iacebo.

Again, what made our poet change the traditional myth? This time, the spell of Propertius' Cynthia, I would suggest. Although just buried, Cynthia makes a surprise visit to the poet's bedchamber during the night, and *leans over his bed* (Prop. 4.7.1-6):

Sunt aliquid Manes: letum non omnia finit,
luridaque evictos effugit *umbra* rogos.

Cynthia namque meo visa est incumbere fulcro,
    murmur ad extremae nuper humata viae,
cum mihi somnus ab exsequiis penderet amoris,
    et quererer lecti frigida regna mei.

I think, out of this innocent *incumbere fulcro*, on the part of Cynthia, the wild imagination of the Barcelona bard has made, *veniam tecum<que> iacebo* (90), "I shall come to lie down with you," on the part of Alcestis. This suggestion seems to find support in another encounter between Cynthia and our Alcestis. The latter's words, *Si redeunt umbr<a>e, veniam* (90), seem to echo Cynthia's statement, *Nocte vagae ferimur, nox clausas liberat umbras* (4.7.89).

In conclusion, our poet seems to combine two different motifs—*the effigy* of Alcestis (deriving from Euripides and Ovid), and *the shade* of Alcestis (inspired by Propertius' Cynthia). Take notice of the difference between, *meque puta tecum sub nocte iacere* (86), and, *veniam tecum<que> iacebo* (90). The former derives from Eurip. *Alc.* 351 f.: τὴν φίλην ἐν ἀγκάλαις | δόξω γυναῖκα οὐκ ἔχων ἔχειν. The latter is inspired by Cynthia's words, *Nocte vagae ferimur, nox clausas liberat umbras* (4.7.89). One thing is "to think, imagine" (86: *puta*, δόξω), another thing is "to be present in person" (90: *veniam*, vs. *vagae ferimur*, of Propertius). Again, we are dealing here with two different motifs.

71-82. *Pro coniuge coniux*

71. Pelieïa : This is Hutchinson's emendation of P's unmetrical *peleide*. Compare Verg. *Aen.* 2.403: *Priameïa virgo* (i.e., Cassandra); 3.212 f.: *Phineïa...* | *... domus*; Ovid *Met.* 13.404 and 513: *Priameïa coniunx* (i.e., Hecuba).—Tandoi reads: *Pelieida*, with the remark: "sermo vulgaris, haud aliter ac nomin. *Briseida*, *Laida* etc. apud poetas serioris aevi." But such a *sermo vulgaris* cannot be paralleled in our educated poet.

fletus : For Admetus' endless crying, compare lines 22; 24; 44; 45; 107.

72. | me, <me>... me : Such an emotional anaphora seems to be a Vergilian mannerism: *Aen.* 9.427: | *me, me, adsum qui feci, in me convertite ferrum*; 8.144 f.: *me, me ipse meumque* | *obieci caput*; 12.260 f.: *me, me duce ferrum* | *corripite*.

trade neci : This reading is warmly recommended by *dede neci* in Verg. *Georg.* 4.90; Ovid *Fasti* 4.840; *Heroid.* 14.125. P has, however, *trade niquid*, which Ed., followed by the Oxonienses, reads, *inquit* (while keeping P's *exclamans* in the next line). I feel, however, that the pedestrian *inquit* is uncalled for. First, compare the parallelism between 71-73, *ut talis vidit...,* | *exclamat*, and 122 f., *ut vidit...,* | *exclamat*. Second, our poet does not use *inquit*. Compare: 12 *Pr<a>escius <h>eu P<a>ean*; 25 *Edocet ille patrem*; 32 *Hic genitor*; 46 *haec super inproperans*; finally, 123 *exclamat*. Third, the reading *neci* is supported by the parallelism between *nex* and *mors* in lines 72 (*me trade neci, me... trade sepulcris*) and 81 (*mors ista... me trade sepulcris*). Finally, P's *niquid* seems to be induced by the preceding *inquid*, obviously belonging to the marginal indication, *Alcestis inquit*, since P actually offers here: χ *alcestis me inquid trade niquid*.

In conclusion, P's *niquid* is a heavy corruption of *neci*, written under the influence of the marginal gloss, *inquid*. Our scribe writes *i* for *e* also in lines 48 (*ubira* for *ubera*); 104 (*alis* for *ales*), and elsewhere; and he writes *q* for *c* also in lines 10 (*pe*[[*q*]]`*c´udum*); 18 (*qum ... qum*); 27 (*doquere*); 53 (*quicui*).

trade sepulcris : *C.L.E.* 537.4: *corpus... tradi sepulcro* |; Lucan 4.737 f.: *leti fortuna propinqui | tradiderat fatis iuvenem*; Claudian *De Raptu Pros.* 2.251 f.: *sic me crudelibus umbris | tradere*. Apparently, Alcestis deliberately repeats the injunction, *me trade sepulcris*, at the opening (72) and closing (81) of her argument. The poet wants to demonstrate the determination of the heroine, reflecting her noble *pietas*.

73. libens : A perfect *stellvertretendes Opfer* should offer itself gladly and of free will. Compare Hygin. *Fab.* 51.3: *Et illud ab Apolline accepit* [sc. Admetus], *ut pro se alius voluntarie moreretur. Pro quo cum neque pater neque mater mori voluisset, uxor se Alcestis obtulit et pro se vicaria morte interiit*; Apollodor. *Bibl.* 1.9.15.2: ἂν ἑκουσίως τις ὑπὲρ αὐτοῦ θνῄσκειν ἕληται; infra, v. 110: *l<a>eta*.

ego tempora dono | : This matches Admetus' request addressed to Pheres, *si tempora dones* | (29).

74. <e>ventura : "Admetus, I gladly donate my *coming* days to you!" The phrase most probably alludes to the motif of "the tantamount life-span," already mentioned in line 17, *tu poteris posthac alieno vivere fato*. The motif seems to have been present in the Alcestis myth, ἵνα ἴσον τῷ προτέρῳ χρόνον ζήσῃ (see ad v. 17).

pro coniuge coniux | : This clear Ovidian borrowing serves to our poet as a *motto* for his heroine: *Met.* 7.589 f.: *quotiens pro coniuge coniunx, | pro gnato genitor...*; 11.660: *inveniesque tuo pro coniuge coniugis umbram*; *Heroid.* 3.37: *... (sed non opus est tibi coniuge) coniunx* | *...* For such a polyptoton compare, e.g., Hesiod *Theog.* 380, θεὰ θεῷ (et saepius), and M. L. West, p. 76.

75. vinco pietate parentem | : Statius *Silvae* 2.1.96: *Quid referam altricum victas pietate parentes?*; Silius 16.474: *trepidi pietate parentes* |; *C.L.E.* 249.20 and 475.1: *pietate parentis* |; Martial 5.28.3: *pietate fratres Curvios licet vincas*.

76. | si m < or > ior : Stat. *Theb.* 1.661: | *dum morior.*

laus magna mei : Cf. Eurip. *Alc.* 623 f.: πάσαις δ' ἔθηκεν εὐκλεέστερον βίον | γυναιξίν; *Alcesta* 154: *aeternam moriens famam* [= *Aen.* 7.2] *tam certa tulisti* [= 9.249] (sc. Alcestis).—*laus mei* for *laus mea* : cf. Hofmann-Szantyr, *Lat. Syntax*² 61 β.

laus magna mei post funera nostra : The change from singular to plural is poetic. Consequently, *nostra* should be kept in the text. Compare infra, 86 f.: *me cole, meque puta...* | *... cineres nostros*; Propert. 1.1.33: *in me nostra Venus* (and M. Rothstein, ad loc.; Lebek 26).

funera nostra : Propert. 2.1.55 f.:

> una meos quoniam praedata est femina sensus,
> ex hac ducentur funera nostra domo.

The alliteration of lines 74-76 (74: *c- c-*; 75: *v- m- v- p- p-*; 76: *m- l- m- m- n-*) seems to be here to witness to the firm resolve of the heroine.

77. totis narrabitur annis | : Ovid *Met.* 14.435: *Talia multa mihi longum narrata per annum*; 730 f.: | *Este mei memores...* | *... et longo facite ut narremur in aevo*; *C.L.E.* 249.19: *accipe, posteritas, quod per tua saecula narres*; 1216.10 f.: | *et memores nostri nostrorumque alta propago* | *aeterno servent semper memorabile nomen*; Statius *Silvae* 3.2.135: *medios narrabimus annos* |.

78. coniux pia : Ovid. *Met.* 13.301: *Me pia detinuit coniunx, pia mater Achillem*; Seneca *Troades* 501: *coniugis ... piae* |; *C.L.E.* 557.1: *Aurelia Pia piissima coniux* |; 555.1 = 556.1: *pientissima coniux* |.

tristior atros | : The comparative is employed *metri gratia*: Ovid *Trist.* 4.8.3: *Iam subeunt anni fragiles et inertior aetas* |; Catull. 3.2: *et quantum est hominum venustiorum* |; Martial 4.86.7: *nec rhonchos metues maligniorum* |; 5.2.3 f.: *tu, quem nequitiae procaciores* | *delectant nimium.* Cf. Hofmann-Szantyr, *Lat. Syntax*² 169.—The presence of such an "empty comparative," employed *metri gratia* at the closing of a line, does not mean that the comparatives, | *dulcior*, and | *carior*, employed at the beginning of lines 84 and 85, had lost their comparative sense as well. All the contrary, they express Alcestis' last wish addressed to her husband—to remain, in his heart, as a greater *love* than any future wife of his.

In view of this, P's *tristior* should not be changed into *tristis.*

79. non tristior atros | **aspiciam vultus** : Since the future tenses, (79) *aspiciam... flebo*, and (80) *servabo*, evidently refer to Alcestis' possible life as a *widow*, I would understand the clause to mean, "I shall not have to look at the sullen (gloomy, somber) faces (of your parents and our children) around me for the rest of my life." I think the verb *aspiciam* speaks in favor of P's *vultus* (not Nisbet's *cultus*). Most probably, these "sullen faces" belong to the members of Admetus' family. Lebek, however, takes it to refer to Admetus, while translating. "Nicht werde ich traurig deine russgeschwärzten Züge anschauen." This is not likely to me.

However, the expression, *atri vultus*, in the sense of "sullen faces," is difficult to parallel. Compare perhaps Seneca *Herc. Furens* 694: *aterque Luctus*; Silius 2.549 f.: *tunc Luctus et atri | pectora circumstant Planctus Maerorque Dolorque*; Horace *Epist.* 1.19.12: *vultu torvo*. The juxtaposition, *tristior atros*, seems to speak in favor of the sense, "sullen, gloomy," (not "unfriendly"), for *ater*.

toto tempore flebo | : "I shall not weep *each time* I attend to your ashes" (*toto = omni*). Compare Ovid *Pont.* 3.1.103: *Utque meae res sunt, omni, puto, tempore flebis |*.

Take notice of the alliteration of *t* in lines 78-80, attesting to the *tristesse* of Alcestis as a widow. (For a similar effect of *t* compare line 39.)

80. dum cineres servabo tuos : In the script of P (and in the old cursive script), the letters *d* and *a* look similar (compare, e.g., the word *dea* in line 67). Hence the corruption in P: *dum > aum > aut* (a similar corruption is present in 68: *dum > aum > aut > et* P).—*servabo* stands here for *observabo* (*O.L.D.*, s.v., 4a): Ovid *Fasti* 6.317: *Inde focum servat pistor dominamque focorum*; Curtius 4.10.23: *omnem... honorem funeri patrio Persarum more servavit* (sc. Alexander).

82. me portet... Po<r>t<h>meus : "let *me* be carried away by the Carrier!" Alcestis closes her argument with a reference to Charon, while being careful not to mention his name. At the same time, she employs an elegant *paronomasia*. Lebek (26) correctly referred to *C.L.E.* 1223.7: *portabit Portitor*. For *Porthmeus = portitor Charon* compare Petronius 121 v.117; Juvenal 3.266; *C.L.E.* 1549.3.

nigro velamine : Ovid *Met.* 11.611: *pullo velamine tectus |*.

83-92. *On revient toujours à ses premières amours*

83. | Hoc tantum : Silius 6.501 f. (Marcia to Regulus): *| Hoc unum, coniux, uteri per pignora nostri | unum oro*; *Iliad* 1.504: τόδε μοι κρήηνον ἐέλδωρ. "One wish only"—a common formula in prayers and supplications.

moritura rogo : Cf. Eurip. *Alc.* 299 f.: εἶεν· σὺ νῦν μοι τῶνδ' ἀπόμνησαι χάριν· | αἰτήσομαι γάρ σ'...; 308: αἰτοῦμαί σ' ἐγώ |; *Alcesta* 124: *adiuro* (sc. *te*) [= *Aen.* 12.816] *et repetens iterumque iterumque monebo* [= 3.436].

84-85. | dulcior ulla (sc. mulier) tibi, ... coniux | carior : "After I am gone, may you never love another *woman* as much as you did me! May *the wife* to take my place (in your house) never be dearer to your *heart* than I have been!"—This seems to be the most natural interpretation of the text. Lebek, however, punctuates: *vestigia ne mea, coniux, | carior...*, while understanding *coniux* as "Gatte", "my husband" (i.e., Admetus). This is not likely to me. For, first, there is the contrast between (84) *coniux* and (85) *Et tu* (sc. *Admete*). It can be explained only if we take that *coniux* here means "wife" (and not "husband"), in opposition to the allocution, *Et tu*, "As for you, Admetus." Second, even if we understand *coniux* as "you, my husband," there will still remain *ulla* (sc. *mulier*) in the text, to refer to a possible second wife for Admetus.

Third, the comparatives, (84) | *dulcior*, and (85) | *carior*, witness to the fact that we are dealing here with *two* women who are being compared to each other as objects of Admetus' love. Fourth, by understanding *coniux* as "my husband," the prospect of a second wife for Admetus will not go away. Such a prospect is present also in the vivid picture of a *stepmother* (*noverca*) for Alcestis' orphans, in line 98, and in the final injunction of the heroine, addressed to her husband, *Et tu pro coniuge cara*, "And you too, Admetus, learn to die for your (future) dear wife...!," in lines 102-103 (compare also p. 66 f.). Finally, the possibility of a second marriage for Admetus is supported both by Euripides (*Alc.* 181: σὲ δ' ἄλλη τις γυνὴ κεκτήσεται) and by Cornelia's words addressed to Paullus (Propertius 4.11.85-90).

In conclusion, our Alcestis is not asking her husband never to marry again: her only request for Admetus is to keep her in his heart as his first and greatest love.

vestigia ne mea... | **... legat** : Verg. *Aen.* 9.392 f.: Ovid *Met.* 3.17 [and Fr. Bömer ad loc.]; Lucan 8.210; Statius *Theb.* 9.171; Valer. Flaccus 1.711.

85. ne<c> nomine tantum : "Not in name only." The expression, *nomine* (as opposed to *re*), in the sense of "nominally (not in fact)," sounds pedestrian [cf. *O.L.D.*, s.v., 16b].

86. tecum sub nocte iacere | : The idea recurs in line 90: *tecum<que> iacebo*. Why this repetition? As already suggested earlier (70-72), I think it is due to the fact that the poet is employing two different motifs here. In line 86, he has in mind an *effigy* of Alcestis, made for Admetus by the sculptors (= *cineres nostros*, 87). This motif he took over from Euripides (*Alc.* 348-352), just as Propertius did (4.11.82 f.). But the effigy is not a real Alcestis: hence the phrase, *meque puta* (86), probably echoing Euripides' line 352: δόξω γυναῖκα καίπερ οὐκ ἔχων ἔχειν.

In line 90, however, the poet is referring to a visit by the *shade* (*umbra*) of Alcestis to his bedchamber during the night. This motif he took over from Propertius' Cynthia (4.7.1-6). Since a shade is not the same as an effigy, this time he employs *veniam* (90), not *meque puta* (86)—"I shall come in person."

Still, there is no idea of *tecum sub nocte iacere* either in Euripides or in Propertius. My impression is that the vivid imagination of the Barcelona bard is exploiting and expanding here the ideas found in Euripides (350-352: καὶ περιπτύσσων χέρας | ... τὴν φίλην ἐν ἀγκάλαις | δόξω γυναῖκα... ἔχειν |) and in Ovid's Laodamia story (*Heroid.* 13.154: *amplexus accipit illa* [sc. *cera Protesilai*] *meos*).

87. in gremio cineres nostros : The word *cineres* is a poetic metaphor here standing for an *effigy* of Alcestis (Eurip. *Alc.* 348-352). Most probably, it is not a full-size statue but a smaller one, enabling Admetus to take it into his lap (*gremium*). In so doing, he is only following the example of Ovid's Laodamia (*Heroid.* 13.157: *Hanc* [sc. *ceram Protesiliai*] *specto teneoque sinu pro coniuge vero*). The real ashes of Alcestis (88, *favillae*) will never be in Admetus' bedchamber: the urn with her ashes will be placed in a vault of her grave (89, *titulus*) in the cemetery.

88. nec timida tractare manu : Cf. Martial 14.30.2: *sit modo firma manus* |; Eurip. *Alc.* 350: καὶ περιπτύσσων χέρας; Statius *Theb.* 4.450: | *ipse manu tractans*; 11.658: *regimenque manu tractare cruentum* |; *Silvae* 5.1.87 f.: *viresque modosque* | *imperii tractare manu*; infra, v.118: | *tractavitque manu*.

88-89. sudare fa<v>il<l>as | unguento : "Take care that the urn with my ashes (always) sweats with oil!" With this injunction of Alcestis, and with the following one ("and gird my tombstone with fresh flowers!"), our attention turns from Admetus' *bedchamber* (where he is expected to take Alcestis' effigy into his lap) to the grave (*titulus*) of the deceased wife in the *cemetery*.

Admetus is the subject of the verbs, (87) *tenere*, (88) *tractare manu*, *sudare*, and (89) *pr<a>ecingere*. Accordingly, *sudare* must have been employed here as *transitive*—"to *make* my ashes sweat with oil," "to soak them with sweat" (cf. *O.L.D.*, s.v. *sudo*, 1c). But such a transitive usage of the verb, in this sense, is difficult to parallel, unless it is present in Quintilian *Inst.* 11.3.23: *et in sudata veste durandum*, "stick to your work though your clothes be dripping with sweat," "schweissdurchtränktes Gewand" (Lebek 26).

That is the reason why the Oxonienses change P's text, *sudare failas unguentum*, into, *stillare favillis* [*favillis* already *Ed.*] *unguentum*. I prefer, however, to keep *sudare* in the text for the following reasons. First, palaeographically, it is a lesser risk to change *unguentum* into *unguento*, than to change first *sudare* into *stillare*, and then *favillas* into *favillis*, especially in view of the fact that our scribe writes, e.g., in 2 *tuus* (for *tuo*), in 121 *gremio* (for *gremium*). Second, Statius and Silius do employ *sudare* as transitive, although in a different sense, "to perform/execute with much exertion or sweating" (*O.L.D.*, s.v., 2b): *Thebaid* 4.722; 5.189; *Punica* 3.92; 4.434. Maybe our poet is following Statius and Silius here in employing *sudare* as transitive, while following Vergil in using the same verb as intransitive, in line 113? He has already surprised us with the hapax *egenerare* in line 59.

As for the idea itself, compare Ovid *Fasti* 3.561: *bibunt molles... unguenta favillae* |; *Alcesta* 147 (Admetus speaking): *semper celebrabere donis* | [= *Aen.* 8.76]; 149: *Ipse tibi ad tua templa feram sollemnia dona* [= 9.626]; *C.L.E.* 1256.4-6:

> Vos precor hoc, superi, ut vitam servetis amicis,
> ut possint *nostris Bacchum miscere favillis,*
> *floribus et spargant* saepius *umbra(m)* levem.

89. titulumque : First, a sepulchral inscription (cf. Juvenal 6.230: *titulo res digna sepulchri*), then, as a *synecdoche*, "a tombstone," as is the case here.

novo pr < a > ecingere flore : "and gird my tombstone with ever fresh flowers!" Evidently, Alcestis is obsessed with the idea that her young husband may forget her completely after her death. Hence her injunctions: (91) *coniux, ne desera < r > a te*; (100) *Si tibi dissimuler...* Hence also her request for a *regular cult* to the noble deceased wife: "pour much oil over my ashes" (88 f.); "bring always fresh flowers to my tombstone" (89); and especially, "mourn aloud for me on a regular basis" (*plangere saepe iubet sese*, 108).

But the point is that her requests are at home in the popular sepulchral poetry (just as was her pun of line 82, *me portet melius... Porthmeus*). Compare *C.L.E.* 1256.4-6 (quoted ad vv. 88-89 s.f.); 451.3: | *Sit tibi terra levis, cineres quoque flore tegantur*; 492.20 f.: *ac precor et tu* | *hanc tituli sedem velles decorare quodannis...*; 578.2: | *vicinas mihi carpe rosas, mihi lilia pone...*; 966.3 f.: | *tum tibi si qua mei fatorum cura manebit,* | *ne grave sit tumulum visere saepe meum* [= 965.4]; 1036.9 f.: | *ut sint qui cineres nostros bene floribus sertis* | *saepe ornent.*

pr < a > ecingere flore : Cf. Ovid *Heroid.* 4.71: *praecincti flore capilli* |; *Trist.* 3.13.15: *Fumida cingatur florentibus ara coronis*; Statius *Silvae* 4.8.9: *sertis altaria cingat* |.

90. veniam tecum < que > iacebo | : P offers: *ueniam tecum sub nocte iacebo*. One can restore the meter by sacrificing *veniam* and keeping *sub nocte* (as *Ed.* and Lebek did): *Si redeunt umbr < a > e, tecum sub nocte iacebo*. I prefer, however, to keep *veniam* and sacrifice *sub nocte* as a dittography. The scribe repeated *sub nocte* in 90 for the phrase of line 86, *tecum sub nocte iacere*, was still present in his memory. But in line 86, the words *sub nocte* are necessary, while in 90 they are not, since the clause, *si redeunt umbrae* ("if it is true that the shades of the dead return..."), already implies the idea, "during the night" (the ghosts do not leave Hades during the day).

I think the direct source for the idea, *si redeunt umbrae*, is the statement of Cynthia (Propert. 4.7.89): *Nocte vagae ferimur, nox clausas liberat umbras*. Euripides' *Alcestis rediviva* (1127 f.) could not serve as such a source of inspiration, since she is *not* a phantom (*umbra*).

As for the strange idea of *veniam tecum<que> iacebo*, as already suggested on p. 71 f., it too comes from Propertius' Cynthia elegy (4.7.3): *Cynthia* [i.e., *Cynthiae umbra*] *namque meo visa est incumbere fulcro*. In brief, line 90 combines Prop. 4.7.89 and 3.

91. | **qualiscumque tamen :** "Whatever shape I may have then..." seems to resume *umbrae* from the preceding line. At the same time, it is a Propertian mannerism: 1.18.31: | *Sed qualiscumque es...*; 3.21.16: | *qualiscumque mihi tuque, puella, vale!*; 3.1.30: | *qualemcumque Parim vix sua nosset humus*; 3.23.9: | *qualesumque mihi semper mansere fideles*; Ovid *Amores* 1.6.71: | *Qualiscumque vale*.

ne desera<r> a te | **:** I think our poet is deliberately repeating *desero* in the next line. Alcestis seems to be making the following point: "My husband, never *leave my shadow*! Remember that I have *left the daylight* for you!" In other words, never forget that I have become a shadow because of you. The pun is enhanced by the parallelism between *a te* | (91) and *pro te* | (92), and by the alliteration (92: *doleam de me*, matching *desero pro te* and *desera<r> a te*).

93-103. *Pia pignora and Disce mori*

The last "block" of Alcestis' *rhesis* comprises four important elements. First, following the examples of Euripides' Alcestis and Propertius' Cornelia, the *pia mater* (cf. 99) emphatically and solemnly entrusts her husband with their common children, entreating him to take good care of her small orphans in case he brings a stepmother into the house (93-95 and 98 f.). Second, Alcestis expresses her firm belief that she shall not perish completely: she shall continue to live in the persons of her children who *resemble their mother* so much (96 f.). Third, Alcestis produces a *sanctio*: she threatens Admetus with the revenge and punishment of an abandoned wife, in case he forgets her completely after her self-denying death (100 f.; the apodosis of the sentence is lost). Finally, in her *peroratio*, the heroine delivers a moral injunction addressed to her husband for his possible second marriage (and to all marriageable readers of this *ethopoeia*): "Learn to die for your wife, learn from my example what a sense of duty (*pietas*) is!" (102 f.).

Now, it is amazing to learn that, in these few lines, our *poeta doctus* was able to accommodate borrowings coming from Euripides, Vergil, Horace, Propertius, Ovid, Silius, Statius, Latin sepulchral poetry, and popular folklore as well.

93. | **ante omnes :** Verg. *Aen.* 5.406 et saepius (total, twelve times).

commendo tibi pia pignora natos | : This is a centonic borrowing from Prop. 4.11.73: *Nunc tibi commendo communia pignora natos.* Our poet did not like the expression, *communia pignora* (which is present also in Ovid *Met.* 5.523 f.: *commune est pignus onusque* | *nata mihi tecum*), so he replaced it with *pia pignora.* The clausula, *pia pignora, nati,* | recurs in Dracontius *Romulea* 6.56 (and may well be sepulchral in origin). Another possibility is that our poet wanted to bring Alcestis' children as close to their mother as possible; if so, then *pia pignora* would echo *coniux pia* (78) and *matris pia... umbra* (99)—such mother, such children! Compare 97: *quae mihi tam similes natos moritura relinquo.*

natos : This word here—as well as in lines 19, 97, and 108—probably means, "children," and not "sons." For reportedly Alcestis had four children with Admetus: Eumelus, Perimele, Hippasus, and Pheres (cf. RE I, 378). In Euripides, probably only one son (*Alc.* 311; 393-403; 406-415) and one daughter of Alcestis (313-319) appear on stage (in accordance with a convention of Greek theater).

94. pignora, quae solo de te fecunda creavi : What Alcestis seems to be saying here is that she was a virgin when marrying Admetus, and not a widow or a divorcee with children. In other words, she stresses the fact that Admetus is the only father of all her children (and her only husband). This seems to be another borrowing from the *regina elegiarum,* where Cornelia pointedly states: *in lapide hoc uni nupta fuisse legar* (Prop. 4.11.36), and: *fac teneas unum nos imitata virum* (4.11.68). Another possibility is that our poet, here as well as throughout his *ethopoeia,* simply follows the pattern of the sepulchral poetry. Compare *C.L.E.* 1038.6: *diceris coniunx una fuisse viri*; 1306.4: *Celsino nupta univira unanimis.*

95. ex te sic nullas habe<a>t mors ista querellas : "I have borne you children (94, *pignora... creavi*), so that (*sic*) this premature death of mine (*mors ista*) may find no complaint on your part (*ex te*)." In other words, I have fulfilled my *maternal* duty in our marriage, I have borne you heirs. Similar idea seems to be expressed in *C.L.E.* 492.5 f.:

> Fatorum cursus properans me orbavit ab illo [sc. *coniuge*],
> sic tamen ut pignus dederim *pro corpore corpus.*

P has *de te,* not *ex te.* But the same scribe writes in 62 *de arte* (for *ex arte*), and in 103 *ex me* (for *de me*). Here too, P's *de te* is either a repetition of the *de te* from the preceding line (*de te fecunda*), or was written under the influence of Vulgar Latin (*de te,* for *ex te*). The Oxonienses seem to take 95 *de te* to be a deliberate *anaphora*: *de te fecunda creavi,* | *de te sic...* Shackleton Bailey feels that such an anaphoric *de te* "falls flat, or, worse still, might suggest that the paternity was open to question." He suggests instead: *quae solo de te fecunda creavi* | *de me*: "from you and from me." I am at a loss to see the merits of this emendation.

96. | **Non pereo, nec enim morior** : This clumsy expression seems to be a weak echo of Horace's *Exegi monumentum* ode (*Carm.* 3.30.6): | *Non omnis moriar...*

97. quae mihi tam similes natos : Nisbet's emendation *mihi*, for P's *tibi*, must be correct, since Alcestis is concerned here with *her own survival*: *me, crede, reservo,* | *quae...* Take notice of the *causal* connotation of *quae* (= *ut quae*). P's *tibi tam similes* may have been written under the influence of 100: *si tibi dissimiles* P.

98. man<u>s indigna<nda> novercae : The unworthy *hand* of a stepmother may well derive directly from Euripides, *Alc.* 307: τοῖς σοῖσι χἀμοῖς παισὶ χεῖρα προσβαλεῖ [sc. μητρυιά], while the prospect of an evil stepmother herself is a combination of Euripides (*Alc.* 305-310) and Propertius 4.11.85-90 (quoted on pp. 66 and 68, respectively).

99. prodat, et <h>eu : This is my tentative reading for P's *proderentet*, which I take to be a heavy corruption. A subjunctive present is warmly recommended here by the presence of *vindicet*; so is a consecutive *et* between the two verbs. Finally, *<h>eu* (cf. v. 12) is welcome in view of both *flentes* and *vindicet*. If so, then the reading, *prodat, et <h>eu*, seems to be the best candidate for P's *proderentet*. The process of corruption seems to have been as follows: *prodat et eu* (*eu* for *<h>eu* also in line 12) > *prodet et en* > *prodet en et* > *proderent et*. The scribe writes *e* for *a* also in lines 91, *desere* (for *deser<a>r*); 76, *funere* (for *funera*); 10, *crimine* (for *crimina*). But *proderent* seems to be a deliberate improvisation for the illegible *prodat et.*

Whatever the case, the verb *prodat* seems to offer a better sense ("may she not betray the trust of her stepchildren!") than Nisbet's *verberet* or Watt's *proterat*. *Ed.* and Lebek, however, read: *proderet et* (for the infraction of *consecutio temporum* Lebek 26 refers to Hofmann-Szantyr, *Lat. Syntax*², 552). This is less likely to me.

flentes matris pia vindicet umbra : As already suggested (p. 69), the idea of "the crying orphans" and "the avenging dead mother" is absent in both Euripides and Propertius. Most probably it comes from the popular folkloric motif of the faithful dead mother *avenging* her maltreated orphans *even from her grave* (literature on p. 69).

pia... umbra | : Cf. Propert. 3.18.31: *pias hominum... umbras* |; 4.11.74: *haec cura et cineri spirat inusta meo.*

100. Si tibi dissimuler : "If you neglect me," "if you deliberately disregard me (after my death)..." This is von Albrecht's improvement of my reading, *si me dissimules*. It is closer to P's text: *si tibi dissimiles*. The Oxonienses read, *si mihi dissimiles*, while Lebek keeps, *si tibi dissimiles.*— Compare Ovid *Pont.* 1.2.146: *non potes hanc salva dissimulare fide.*

si non mea dulcis imago | paulum ad te veni < at > : "if the sweet image of me does not come to your mind from time to time..." I share with Hutchinson the need for the change of P's *hoc* into *si*. This *hoc* is the fruit of a wild imagination, on the part of the scribe, who had misunderstood his exemplar. He took *si tibi dissimules* of his corrupt exemplar to mean, "if you ignore this request of mine," i.e., *quos, rogo, ne parvos man < u > s indigna < nda > novercae | prodat* (98 f.). Consequently, he replaced *si* with *hoc*, to refer to Alcestis' request concerning her orphans. This request, however, ends with the impressive phrase of 99, *et < h > eu flentes matris pia vindicet umbra*. With line 100, Alcestis turns to a different subject, to her own image in the memory of her husband, as the expression, *mea dulcis imago*, attests.

On the other hand, the anaphora of *si* is necessary as part of the σχῆμα καθ' ὅλον καὶ μέρος (present also in line 118). For the absence of the sweet image of Alcestis in the memory of her husband (*si non mea dulcis imago | paulum ad te veni < at >*) is only *one example* of the general attitude, on the part of Admetus, "if you neglect me" (*si tibi dissimuler*).

Lebek, however, keeps the text as transmitted, while translating: "Wenn du dir dies vernachlässigen solltest, dann kommt nicht mein süsses Bild ein wenig in der Nacht." This interpretation is not likely to me for the following reasons. First, thematically, "the sweet image of me" has nothing to do with the image of Alcestis' orphans being maltreated by an evil stepmother. Again, her request about her children ends with *matris... umbra*, of line 99. Second, the clause, *non mea dulcis imago | paulum nocte venit* (as Lebek reads), cannot serve as an apodosis to the protasis, *si tibi dissimiles hoc*, for the simple reason that the absence of the "sweet image" of Alcestis in the bedchamber of Admetus cannot serve as a credible *punishment*. This is exactly what Alcestis *demands* from her husband—*me cole, meque puta tecum sub nocte iacere* (86)! Third, the text: *si tibi dissimiles hoc, non mea dulcis imago*, does not seem to be a good hexameter. Finally, P's *hoc* (for *si*) is not the only improvisation on the part of the scribe. Compare also: *si {non} te colui* (9); *{neue} digna retinere* (87); *ueniam tecum {sub nocte} iacebo* (90); *tibi* (for *mihi*, 97) [and *Index of scribal errors*, s. Improvisation].

dulcis imago | : Statius *Silvae* 1.2.112 f.: *mihi dulcis imago | prosiluit*; *Theb.* 5.608: *o mihi desertae natorum dulcis imago*.

101. paulum : "from time to time." Our Alcestis knows well (as does Propertius' Cornelia) that a young widower with small children is likely to remarry soon after her death. In 83-85, she makes the best effort for herself when demanding from her husband to remain *his first and greatest love*, even after his marriage to another woman (*ne post mea fata | dulcior ulla tibi, vestigia ne mea coniux | carior ista legat*, 83-85). In 101 she is more realistic when demanding much less—that her husband recalls the sweet image of his dead wife *from time to time*. The same ambivalence seems to be present already in the Euripidean Alcestis (contrast *Alc.* 181 to 305-310 and 371 f.).

ad te veni<at>... | ... Et tu : "if the sweet image of me does not come *to your mind* from time to time..." Statius' expression, *mihi dulcis imago | prosiluit*, suggests that *ad te* is necessary here to convey the idea of "comes to your mind." P has, however, *nate* or *note*, which all read as *no<c>te* (with the exception of Parsons, who suggests *nota*). But P's *nate* seems to be a corruption of *ad te*, due to the similarity between *a* and *d* in the old cursive script (compare 80: *dum : aut* P)—*adte> aate*. Then the scribe converted this *aate* into *nate* to make some sense, probably under the influence of the allocution, *nate*, in lines 34, 41, 51, and 56 as well.

veni<at>... et : This *subiunctivus potentialis* (*si non veni<at>*) is recommended here by the same subjunctive in 100, *si tibi dissimuler*. P has, however, *ueniet* (for *veni<at>... et*), which Lebek and Parsons read: *veni<t>. Et*, and, *veni<t>, et*, respectively (*sine lacuna*).

The **lacuna :** After a double protasis—*si tibi dissimuler, si non mea dulcis imago| paulum ad te veni<at>*—we badly need an apodosis, which is, however, missing in our text. Hence the necessity to assume a lacuna here. Most probably, it comprised a threat of *revenge*, on the part of the forgotten noble wife (for example, "then I shall come to haunt you"). The idea of a revenge is already present in the neighboring line 99 (*vindicet*). As for the image of an abandoned and forgotten wife, the example of Dido comes to mind. Compare Verg. *Aen.* 4.384-386 (Dido to Aeneas):

> *Sequar* atris ignibus absens
> et, cum frigida mors anima seduxerit artus,
> *omnibus umbra locis adero*. Dabis, improbe, poenas.

While this suggestion must remain a sheer guess, the fact is that Dido's presence is unmistakable in the following lines 104-107, and that the *shade* of Alcestis was mentioned twice in the preceding lines (90 and 99). One thing, however, seems to be certain: the necessity of a lacuna between *veni<at>* and *et tu*. It need not be longer than, say, one line, and probably was caused by the presence of the same verb in two consecutive lines (e.g., *ad te veni<at>... | ...<veniam>*).

102. ... et tu : Almost certainly, it refers to Admetus, just as the allocution of 85, *et tu*, does. There the adversative *et tu* was caused by the transition from Admetus' second wife (*coniux*, 84) to Admetus himself (*me cole*, 86). Here, the same allocution was probably caused by the transition from "the shade of Alcestis" (in the lacuna) to Admetus. It is Admetus who needs a final moral instruction—on the part of his pious noble wife.

The prospect of a second wife for Admetus is constantly present in Alcestis' mind. While her first request—*rogo* of line 83—deals with the relationship between *Alcestis herself* and the second wife of Admetus (*coniux* of line 84), her second request—*rogo* of line 98—deals with the relationship between *Alcestis' orphans* and the same second wife (*noverca* of line 98). In her *peroratio*, however, the heroine goes one step further: she touches the relationship between *Admetus* and his second wife (102 f.): *Et tu pro coniuge cara* | *disce mori, de m<e> disce exemplu<m> pietatis* ("And you too, Admetus, learn to die for your (new) dear wife! Learn from my example what a sense of (family) duty is!" So far-reaching is the *pietas* of the heroine of this *ethopoeia*!

pro coniuge cara | : The expression reflects the *motto* of the poem—*pro coniuge coniux* (74), with the implication: "In the same way in which I have fulfilled my marital duty by giving my life for my spouse, so you too, Admetus, should learn to do the same (if need be) for your future spouse." But *coniuge cara* | is a stereotyped clausula in sepulchral poetry: *C.L.E.* 490.3: *En cuantus dolor est amissa coniuge cara*; 452.1: *...felix cum coniuge caro* | . The same is true of the expression of 122, *dulcissime coniux* | .

103. disce mori, de m<e> disce exemplu<m> pietatis : *Ed.* was right when referring to Silius' *Punica* 5.636-639 as the direct source of inspiration for our poet, who simply puts the words of Flaminius into the mouth of his Alcestis:

636   sta, miles, et acris
        disce ex me pugnas; vel, si pugnare negatum,
        disce mori: dabit *exemplum* non vile futuris
        Flaminius.

All the words of line 103 are present in Silius, with the only exception of *pietas*, which is an original invention of our poet.

P offers: *disceexmexempla.* Nisbet's reading, *de me<e> disce exemplu<m>*, seems to be preferable to other solutions. Apparently, the scribe had changed the elegant *chiastic* word-order, *disce mori, de me disce*, into the more common one, *disce mori, disce ex me.* (In Silius, the two injunctions belong to the beginning of two consecutive lines, not to one single line.) Moreover, the scribe confounds *de* and *ex* also in lines 62 and 95. And finally, Silius has *exemplum*, not *exempla* (as in P). Alcestis too is offering one single example of her *pietas*—her self-denying death.

In the same vein in which the other contestant in this *Agon*, Clymene, employs a kind of *Ringcomposition* while closing her *rhesis* with a forceful statement expressing the inevitability of death (69: *cedunt labuntur moriun-*

tur contumulantur), which, at the same time, was her opening statement (53: *Cur metui<s> mortem, cui nascimur?*, and 57: *Perpetuum nihil est*), so also Alcestis chooses to close her *anti-rhesis* with her own key-idea (103: *exemplum pietatis*), which, at the same time, had made her opening argument (75: *Si vinco matrem, vinco pietate parentem...*).

104-124. *The last day of the heroine and her tragic death*

The last twenty lines (or so) of the poem depict in brief but powerful terms the last day of life of the heroine (104-116), and her noble death (117-124). She spends the last night of her life with her beloved husband in their bedchamber. Nobody sleeps, nobody talks: he keeps weeping, she keeps staring at him, as if wishing to imprint his image in her memory forever (104-107). Tomorrow morning, Alcestis bids both her husband and her children not to neglect the ritual but rather to mourn aloud for the deceased wife and mother on a regular basis. She takes care of her personal servants in her last will, and, above all, she herself engages in the preparations of her own funeral pyre. Cheerful in her heart, she *personally* collects and prepares all the exotic plants, aromatic spices, unguents and frankincense which are necessary for the cremation of the body on the pyre (108-116).

The process of death of the heroine is described in eight short but effective lines (117-124). Alcestis dies *slowly*, just as one who had drunk hemlock. Now, *more poetarum tragicorum*, the Euripidean Alcestis dies slowly (203: φθίνει γὰρ καὶ μαραίνεται νόσῳ) so that she may talk while on stage and engage in the last and touching *stichomythia* with Admetus (374-391). For a similar reason, our Alcestis too dies slowly in order to address her beloved husband for the last time (122-124, contrasting Euripides' simple χαῖρ' of line 391). The imagination of the Barcelona bard found it necessary to introduce three chthonic deities to deprive the young woman of her daylight: *Hora fatalis* (117); *Mors* (resembling Euripides' *Thanatos*, 123), and an *Infernus deus* (most probably, *Dis pater* or *Pluto*, 124). The *Portitor Porthmeus* was already mentioned in line 82.

104-116. *Ultimus ignis*

104. The scene opens with an unmistakable Vergilian image: "The peaceful Night has arrived, and every living being already sleeps: only not the misfortunate Dido/Alcestis." Compare lines 104-107 with *Aen.* 4.522 f. and 529-531:

> *Nox erat* et placidum *carpebant* fessa *soporem*
> corpora per terras...

> *at non* infelix animi *Phoenissa*, neque umquam
> solvitur in somnos oculisve aut pectore noctem
> accipit.

3.147: *Nox erat et terris animalia somnus habebat*; 2.8 f.: *Et iam nox umida caelo | praecipitat suadentque cadentia sidera somnos*; 9.224-227:

> *Cetera* per terras omnis *animalia somno*
> laxabant curas et corda oblita laborum:
> *ductores Teucrum* primi, delecta iuventus
> consilium summis regni de rebus habebant...

vaga... Nox : "The roving Night" seems to be a borrowing from Statius: cf. *Silvae* 3.1.42: *vagae post crimina noctis* | ; *Theb.* 3.63: *noctis vaga lumina testor* | .

sideribus Nox pingebatur : Seneca *Medea* 310: *stellisque quibus pingitur aether* | ; *Thyest.* 834: *et vaga picti sidera mundi* | ; Manilius 1.445: *caelum depingitur astris* | .

ales | ...Somnus | : *A.L.* 273.1 (Modestinus): *Forte iacebat Amor victus puer alite Somno*; Statius *Theb.* 10.302: *Deus aliger* (sc. *Somnus*).

105. rore soporifero... Somnus : Verg. *Aen.* 5.854-856:

> Ecce deus (sc. *Somnus*) ramum Lethaeo *rore* madentem
> vique *soporatum* Stygia super utraque quassat
> tempora (sc. Palinuri), cunctantique natantia lumina solvit.

Ovid *Met.* 11.586: *Vise soporiferam Somni velociter aulam*; Lucan 3.8 f.: *Inde soporifero cesserunt languida somno | membra ducis*; Lucret. 4.453 f.: *Denique cum suavi devinxit membra sopore | somnus* [cf. infra, v. 124]...
   The *r/s* alliteration of line 105 suggests the dropping of the slumber-inducing dew.

omnia : *animalia* can be easily understood from Vergil *Aen.* 9.224 (quoted above). Similarly, in line 118 *membra* is easily understood with *omnia*.

106. in coniuge fixa iacebat | ... videbat | : This clumsy rhyme is here to convey the idea that Alcestis is spending her last night with her husband in their bedchamber, and that neither of them can sleep: he weeps, she gazes at him.

107. lacrimasq < ue > viri : Cf. Eurip. *Alc.* 201: χλαίει (sc. Admetus) γ' ἄκοιτιν ἐν χεροῖν φίλην ἔχων.

peritura videbat | : *peritura* is a metrical "filler," weak in sense. Compare 97: *moritura relinquo* | ; 119 *moritura notabat* | ; and Ovid *Heroid.* 10.119-121 (Ariadne):

> Ergo ego nec *lacrimas matris moritura videbo*,
>   nec, mea qui digitis *lumina condat*, erit;   [cf. v. 19]

spiritus infelix peregrinas *ibit in auras*, [cf. v. 6]
  nec positos artus unguet amica manus.

108. With this line, the *dawn* has arrived; Alcestis leaves the bed-chamber, meets her children and personal servants, and starts preparing her own funeral pyre. Lebek's question (27): "Warum stirbt Alcestis nachts?" is a wrong one. Alcestis does not die during the night. For tomorrow morning, she has first to collect *personally* the balsam from the balsam-tree and to strip off the dry cinnamon from the cinnamon-tree (lines 113 and 115, respectively), which cannot be done during the night.

plangere saepe iubet sese : *saepe* goes with *plangere*, not with *iubet*: "She bids both her husband and her children *often* [i.e., on a regular basis] to mourn aloud for her." Our Alcestis takes every precaution not to be forgotten by her husband and her children after her heroic death. Hence this request, hence also the request that her urn with the ashes always sweats with oil (88 f.: [*dignare*]... *sudare fa<v>il<l>as | unguento*), and that her tombstone be always covered with fresh flowers (89: *titulumque novo pr<a>ecingere flore*). Incidentally, the expression of 89, *novo... flore*, "with *ever* fresh flowers," speaks in favor of the connection, *plangere saepe*, "and *often* mourn aloud for me." The same is confirmed by the sepulchral poetry: *C.L.E.* 682.10: *et siccato saepe madescunt lumina fletu*; 1036.6: *atque obitum nostrum fletibus usque luunt*.

Consequently, *saepe iubet* is sound. Shackleton Bailey's *sed prohibet*, and F. Jones' *saepe vetat*—in addition to being palaeographically violent—contradict the *pietas* and religiosity of the heroine. Shackleton Bailey refers to Propertius 4.11.1: *Desine, Paulle, meum lacrimis urgere sepulcrum*. But there the line is part of a *different* motif, for its pentameter reads: *panditur ad nullas ianua nigra preces*. Incidentally, both Cynthia and Alcestis believe that this gate of Hades will be open for them during the night: *Nocte vagae ferimur, nox clausas liberat umbras* (Propert. 4.7.89) vs. *Si redeunt umbr<a>e, veniam tecum<que> iacebo* (line 90 of our poem).

natosque virumque | : Ovid. *Met.* 6.301 f.: *orba resedit* (sc. Niobe) *| exanimes inter natos natasque virumque.*

109. disponit famulos : I would take it to mean, "she (orally) disposes (or makes willing) concerning her servants," i.e., "she takes care of her servants in her last will." For the sense, διατίθεται, of *disponit* [sc. *in testamento*], compare *T.L.L.* V. 1427.20-27: e.g., *Vulgate 2 Reg.* 17:23: *disposita domo sua... interiit*.

There may be a deliberate contrast between *disponit famulos* and *conponit in ordine funus*: the pious Alcestis first distributes (allots) her personal servants in her last will, and then thinks of her own funeral.

110. la < a > eta sibi : *sibi* goes with *funus* of the preceding line, not with *laeta*. (Plautus *Miles* 387: *ego laeta visa* [sc. *mihi*]; Tacitus *Ann.* 2.26.1: *laetus animi*; Apuleius *Met.* 5.6.7: *laetus animo*, are not adequate parallels.)

Alcestis' heart is cheerful, first, because she is aware of the fact that she is fulfilling her sacred duty as a family-member (*pietas* of lines 75 and 103); second, because a perfect substitute victim should offer itself gladly and of free will [cf. ad v. 73 *libens*]. Lebek's remark (27): "Alcestis ist 'froh' da '*mors ista placet*' (V. 81)," misses the point. For Alcestis' state-ment of line 81, "I prefer this death," is part of a *different* argument: "May the sorrowful life *of a widow* stay away from me!" (80 f.).

pictosque toros : The expression, *picti tori*, "the ornate couch," is a borrowing from Vergil (*Aen.* 1.708; 4.206 f.) or Ovid (*Heroid.* 12.30), but the point is that *torus* means here "bier" or "palliasse," for the corpse to be put on the funeral pyre: *O.L.D.*, s.v., 4b.

variosque pa < ratus > : Being associated with *tori*, in the sense of "funeral bier," the expression most probably means here, "a motley (parti-colored) funeral *coverlet* [or some similar funeral apparel]." Com-pare Tacit. *Ann.* 13.17.1: *Nox eadem necem Britannici et rogum construxit, pro-viso ante funebri paratu, qui modicus fuit*; Verg. *Aen.* 6.220-222:

> Tum membra *toro* defleta reponunt,
> *purpureasque super vestis*, velamina nota,
> coniciunt.

Statius *Silvae* 2.1.159: *quod tibi purpureo tristis rogus aggere crevit...* [and Fr. Vollmer ad loc, p. 331: "Der Scheiterhaufen war mit purpurnen Tep-pichen belegt"]; *Theb.* 6.62 f.: *Tyrioque attollitur ostro | molle supercilium* (speaking of the funeral pyre).

111.† ... ones † | : This lost line provided one verb to go with the accusatives *toros* and *pa < ratus >* of the preceding line, another one to cover the accusatives in the next line, and it also took care of the word-ending (and line-end) -*ones*.

112. barbaricas frondes < et > odores : As is known, funeral plants (especially cypress) are necessary for the decoration of the funeral bier and the pyre. Compare, e.g., Statius *Theb.* 6.54-58:

> Tristibus interea ramis teneraque cupresso
> damnatus flammae torus et puerile feretrum
> texitur: ima virent agresti stramina cultu;
> proxima gramineis operosior area sertis,
> et picturatus morituris floribus agger.

Verg. *Aen.* 4.506 f.: *intenditque locum sertis et fronde coronat | funerea*. Our poet, however, refers here to special, exotic, oriental plants. The phrase, *barbaricas frondes* <*et*> *odores*, is best taken as a *summary* of what is listed in continuation, "eastern plants and perfumes." In view of the expression of line 54, *barbarus ales*, the epithet *barbaricas* seems to be sound, while meaning, "foreign, exotic, oriental." Nisbet's *Arabicas* cannot be correct, for only balsam (myrrh) comes from Arabia.

The poet lists: frankincense (*tus*), saffron-essence (*crocus*), balsam, amomum, and cinnamon. All these five spices and perfumes are to be found in Statius as applied to the funeral pyre. Compare *Silvae* 2.1.159-162:

> Quod tibi purpureo tristis rogus aggere crevit, [cf. v. 110]
> 160 quod Cilicum flores, quod munera graminis Indi,
> quodque Arabes Phariique Palaestinique *liquores*
> arsuram lavere comam.

[The Cilician blooms refer to saffron-essence; the gifts of Indian herbs, to frankincense; *liquores*, to balsam.]; 2.4.34-36: *Assyrio cineres adolentur amomo | et tenues Arabum respirant gramine plumae | Sicaniisque crocis*; 2.6.86-88:

> Odoriferos exhausit flamma Sabaeos
> et Cilicum messes, Phariaeque exempta volucri
> *cinnama* et Assyrio manantes gramine sucos.

[The fragrant harvests of Saba and Cilicia refer to frankincense and saffron-essence, respectively; for the cinnamon stolen from the Pharian bird [i.e., Phoenix], compare infra, ad v. 114.]; 3.3.33-35: *Tu largus Eoa | germina, tu messes Cilicumque Arabumque superbas | merge rogis*; 5.1.210-216:

> 210   Omne illic stipatum examine longo
> ver Arabum Cilicumque fluit floresque Sabaei
> Indorumque arsura seges praereptaque templis
> *tura*, Palaestini simul Hebraeique *liquores*
> Coryciaeque comae Cinyreaque germina; et altis
> 215 ipsa toris Serum Tyrioque umbrata recumbit
> tegmine [cf. v. 110].

5.3.41-43:

> Nam Sicanii non mitius halat
> aura *croci*, dites nec si tibi rara Sabaei
> *cinnama*, odoratas nec Arabs decerpsit *aristas*.

Thebaid 6.59-63 [the preceding text is quoted on p. 88]:

> Tertius adsurgens Arabum strue tollitur ordo
> *Eoas* conplexus *opes* incanaque glebis

tura et ab antiquo durantia *cinnama* Belo.
Summa crepant auro, Tyrioque attollitur ostro
molle supercilium [cf. v. 110]...

tura crocumque : Cf. Verg. *Georg.* 1.56 f.: *Nonne vides, croceos ut
Tmolus odores,* | *India mittit ebur, molles sua tura Sabaei...? Homeric Hymn to
Demeter* 6 [and N. J. Richardson ad loc, p. 142]. For the rest of the
aromatic plants mentioned in our list compare J. André, *Les noms de
plantes dans la Rome antique* (Paris, 1985), s.v.

113. pallida ... balsama : The expression, "the pale balsam-
unguent," is convincing enough in view of Pliny *N.H.* 12.48: *pallidum
amomum*; 13.17: *murrā pallidum (unguentum fit)*; Ovid *Met.* 15.399: *fulva...
murra*: Statius *Silvae* 3.2.141: *candida felices sudent opobalsama virgae*; *T.L.L.*
X. 131.6 ff.

P has, however, *pallada*, which Lebek retains as *Pallada*, "oil." This
is not likely to me. The parallelism between the lines 113 and 115 speaks
in favor of the adjective *pallida*: (113) | *pallida... destringit balsama virga* ≃
| *arida... destringit cinnama ramis*. Either the scribe had mistakenly written
a for *i* (compare 7, *futuri* for *futura*), or rather he is improvising by producing *Pallada* here, just as he did in 66 by writing *Acatem* (for the correct
Agaue).

sudanti destringit balsama virga | : Cf. Verg. *Georg.* 2.118 f.: *Quid
tibi odorato referam sudantia ligno* | *balsama...?*; Statius *Silvae* 3.2.141: *candida
felices sudent opobalsama virgae*; Prudentius *Cathemerinon* 5.115: *... et tenues
crocos*; 117-119: *Illic et gracili balsama surculo* | *desudata fluunt raraque cinnama
| spirant et...*; Justin *Hist.* 36.3.4: *Arbores opobalsami certo anni tempore
balsamum sudant*; Tacit. *Germ.* 45.7: *ubi* [sc. in Oriente] *tura balsamaque
sudantur*; Hieronym. *Epist.* 107.1-2: *ut... viles virgulae balsama pretiosa
sudarent*.

destringit : If the verb is sound, it seems to be employed in lines 113
and 115 in two *different* senses. Since the *gum* balsam is semiliquid, *destringit* probably means here "she rubs" or "scrapes off." Compare,
e.g., Seneca *Epist.* 122.6: *ut... sudorem... destringant*; Martial 14.51.1. On
the contrary, since in line 115 the expression, *arida... cinnama*, refers to
the *dry twigs* (or bark) of cinnamon, *destringit* most probably has now the
sense of "she strips off," or "removes by cutting."

(113) **destringit...**, **(114) percidit...**, **(115) destringit** : The fact that
the heroine *personally* collects and prepares all the spices and perfumes
necessary for her own funeral pyre seems to be of significance. Contrast
Martial 10.97.2: *dum murram et casias flebilis uxor emit*. My guess is that
this is an additional expression of Alcestis' *pietas*. By carefully fulfilling
every religious requirement, the pious heroine wants to approach her
funeral pyre as a *blameless* (τέλειος) *vicaria victima* for her husband.

Although the aromatic plants are necessary for the cremation of a body
to neutralize the smell of the burning flesh (cf. RE III, 355 f., s.v. *Bestat-
tung*), they also serve *religious* purposes. For example, saffron is an old
religious plant, and frankincense (olibanum) is needed as an *apotropaic*
agent. Finally, perfumes and unguents are part of the funeral ritual,
being used to wash and anoint the body of the deceased person.

Catalogues of spices and perfumes abound. Most probably our poet
had used such a catalogue as found in Statius (quoted ad v. 112). However, if Statius' rich lore was not sufficient, he may have been inspired,
e.g., by Ovid *Met.* 10.307-310:

> Sit dives *amomo*,
> *cinnamaque costumque* suum sudataque ligno
> *tura* ferat floresque alios Panchaia tellus,
> 310   dum ferat et *murram*.

Or by Martial 11.54.1-3:

> *Unguenta* et *casias* et olentem funera *murram*
> *turaque* de medio semicremata rogo
> et quae de Stygio rapuisti *cinnama* lecto...

114. ereptum nido : The Oxonienses have correctly referred to Pliny
N.H. 12.85: *Cinnamomum et casias fabulose narravit antiquitas princepsque
Herodotus* [3.111] *avium nidis et privatim... ex inviis rupibus arboribusque
decuti...*; cf. Statius *Silvae* 2.6.87 f.: *Phariaeque exempta volucri* [i.e.,
Phoenici] | *cinnama*.

percidit pulver amomum : "She beats the amomum to powder." P
has *precidit puluer amomi*. But *pr<a>ecidit* cannot yield the required sense
of "she beats to pieces *or* to powder." Hence the need for the easy emendation, *precidit > percidit* (compare the same scribal error in the next
quotation). The sense of "to beat *or* batter" for *percidere* is present, e.g.,
in Plautus' *Casina* 404: *Percide* [Turnebus : *praecide* codd.] *os tu illi odio*;
Seneca *N.Q.* 4b.4.1: *os percidi, non oculi erui solent.*

pulver : The neuter gender is common enough. Lebek (28) referred
to *C.L.E.* 2222 [= *C.I.L.* VIII.7277]: *haec via tale pulver habet; Anon. Med.*
ed. Piechotta 119; *Hippiatr. Gr.* I, pp. 390.21; 419.5.—For the pulverized
amomum, *friatum amomum*, compare Pliny *N.H.* 12.49; Ovid *Trist.*
3.3.69: *amomi pulvere.*

amomum : It makes a double accusative with *pulver: percidit pulver
amomum = amomum pulver facit.* Compare, e.g., *Chiron* 611: *Hippiatr. Gr.*
I, p. 230.10: *ervum molitum... cataplasmam facies; Hofmann-Szantyr, Lat.
Syntax*[2] 46.—The scribal error, *pulver amomi* (for the correct *pulver
amomum*) seems to be a clear case of an improvisation, on the part of the

scribe (compare also, e.g., 7 *vita futuri*, for *vita futura* <*est*>; 13 *mestum*, for *maesti*; 61 *stygium*, for *Stygii*).—For the combination, (114) *amomum*, (115) *cinnama*, compare κιννάμωμον in Pliny *N.H.* 12.86: *si quidem cinnamomum idemque cinnamum nascitur in Aethiopia*.

115. destringit cinnama : "She strips off the dry cinnamon-twigs (bark)." See ad v.113 *destringit*.

116. Alcestis' order for all these spices and perfumes (*omnes... odores*) to be burnt on the pyre along with her body applies to frankincense, amomum and cinnamon only. For the saffron-oil and the balsam-oil will be used to anoint the dead body. Evidently, the line is a poetic brachylogy, where *secum* implies both usages of *odores*.

117-124. *Mors ultima venit*

117. Hora : Simply *Hora*, for *Hora mortis* or *fatalis*, is well established: *T.L.L.* VI.2963.30-57. Its personification in poetry is easily understandable. Compare, e.g., *C.I.L.* V.6710: *si Ora et Fatus dictasset.*—Cf. *C.L.E.* 55.7: *properavit hora tristis fatalis mea*; 389.2: *fatalis me abstulit hora*; 1295.3: *fatalis... hora*; cf. *infra*, v.120: *fatali frigore pressos*.

propinquabat : A Vergilian echo. *Hoc loco: Aen.* 2.730; 5.159; 9.371; 11.621; Silius 9.278; 12.691; 17.605. *Hoc sensu: Aen.* 12.150 = *Alcesta* 46: *Parcarumque dies et vis inimica propinquat*; Statius *Achill.* 1.257 f.: *metuenda propinquant | tempora*; Tacit. *Ann.* 6.28: *ubi mors propinquet*.

lucem ra<p>tura puellae : Compare *C.L.E.* 466.3: *rapta est mihi lux gratissima vitae*; supra, vv.14: *gratamque relinquere lucem |*; 42: *visurus post fata diem*; 50: *hostis mihi lucis |*.

118. tractavitque manu : The Hour of death touches Alcestis with her (cold) hand: at once, numbness starts seizing her every limb. There is a deliberate difference in verbal aspect between *tractavit* and *corripiebat*: the Hour touches Alcestis with her deadly hand *only once*, but the ensuing *process* of numbness spreading throughout her body is a long one.

For the force of "the hand of Death" compare, e.g., Verg. *Aen.* 10.419: *| iniecere manum Parcae*; *C.L.E.* 995.8: *| iniecere manus invida fata mihi*.

P offers: *tractabat quae manos*. In writing *tractabat* (for the correct *tractavit*), the scribe most probably was induced by the imperfects: *propinquabat* (in the preceding line), *diripiebat* (in the same line), *notabat* (in the next line). In line 105 he wrote *complebent* for the correct *conpleve<ra>t*.—As for the scribal error *manos* (for *manu*), compare, e.g., in 45 P's *fletus* (for *fletu*), in 119 P's *oculos* (for *oculis*).

There is no need to look for another verb to replace *tractavit* here, since the expression, *tractare manu*, is well established: compare supra, v.88 *nec timida tractare manu*, and the instances quoted there.

rigor omnia corripiebat : Cf. Silius 4.455 f.: *subitoque trementem | corripuit pallor*; *Alcesta* 133 [= *Aen.* 4.499]: *pallor simul occupat ora.* —With *omnia* the word *membra* is easily understood, as this becomes clear from the words, *ungues* and *pedes*, in the next two lines: it is kind of the σχῆμα καθ' ὅλον καὶ μέρος.—The alliteration of *r* in lines 117-118, reflecting this *rigor mortis*, reverberates in *fatali frigore*, of line 120.

119. c<a>eruleos ungues : Alcestis' fingernails are becoming blue with the *frost* of death. For such a connotation of *caeruleus*, "blue," or rather "dark-colored, dusky," compare, e.g., *Epicedion Drusi* 93: *lumina caerulea iam iamque natantia morte*; Verg. *Georg.* 1.236: | *caeruleae* (sc. *zonae*); Valerius Flacc. 7.563: | *caerulei Boreae ferus horror*; Statius *Silvae* 5.1.128 f.: *pallida Rheni | frigora.*

120. algentisque pedes : Cf. Seneca *N.Q.* 4.5.3: *algent pedes*; Pliny *N.H.* 25.151: *incipiunt algere ab extremitatibus corporis.*

fatali frigore pressos : Lucret. 6.845: | *frigore cum premitur*; Ovid *Ars Amat.* 2.317: | *cum modo frigoribus premitur...*; *Pont.* 1.7.11: *Nos premit aut bello tellus, aut frigore caelum.* —Silius 6.170: *et occulto riguerunt frigore membra* |; 5.527-529:

> tum, *diffundente per artus*
> *frigore* se *Stygio*, manantem in viscera mortem
> accipit et longo componit lumina somno.

Ovid *Heroid.* 9.135 f. (Deianira):

> Mens fugit admonitu, *frigusque perambulat artus*,
> et iacet in gremio *languida facta manus.*

For the alliteration, *fatali frigore*, compare, e.g., Ovid *Met.* 15.54: *fatalia fluminis ora* |; *Pont.* 1.8.64: *Nerunt fatales fortia fila deae* [cf. *supra*, v.4].—As for the scribal error *pressum* (for *pressos*), compare: vv.41 *tumulus* (for *tumulos*); 44 *lacrimum* (for *lacrimas*); 59 *locus* (for *locos*); 78 *atrus* (for *atros*); 110 *pictus* (for *pictos*); 116 *arsurus* (for *arsuros*).—Parsons' *pressa* (for P's *pressum*) is also possible (but I do not like the hiatus, *pressa | Admeti*).

121. | Admeti : This is the name Alcestis keeps in her mind (cf. v.74). Hutchinson's change into *coniugis* is not likely. The poet had found in his sources, *coniugis in gremium*, but he *deliberately* changed it into, *Admeti in gremium*, in order to exploit the touching allocution, *Dulcissime coniux*, in the next line while, at the same time, avoiding unnecessary repetition.

in gremium : The comforting lap of a spouse is an old image, probably going back to Lucretius. Compare Verg. *Georg.* 2.326: | *coniugis in gremium laetae descendit* (sc. Aether Telluris); Lucan 8.106: | *coniugis in gremium* (sc. Cornelia Pompei); Lucret. 1.33 f.: *in gremium qui* (sc. Mavors) *saepe tuum* (sc. Veneris) *se | reicit*; Verg. *Aen.* 8.405 f.: *placidum-*

que petivit (sc. Volcanus) | *coniugis* (sc. Veneris) *infusus gremio per membra soporem* [cf. infra, v.124]; Tibull. 1.1.59 f.:

> Te spectem, suprema mihi cum venerit hora,
> te teneam moriens deficiente manu.

C.L.E. 1138.2: | *optaram in manibus coniugis occidere.*

refugit fugientis imago | : Verg. *Aen.* 10.656: *Aeneae fugientis imago* |; Silius 17.644: *Hannibalis campis fugientis imago*|. The poet seems to be conveying two ideas here: (1) At this point, Alcestis is only "a fleeting shadow," i.e., the shadow of a living being passing away. The idea of "an illusory apparition, phantom, or mental picture" is present in *imago* both in Vergil and Silius. And (2), this "fleeing soul" is seeking refuge exactly in the lap of her beloved husband; hence the pun *refugit fugientis*. The fact, however, remains that *fugientis imago* is a slavish borrowing.

122. ut vidit : "When she felt (perceived)..." The verb can yield a satisfactory sense, so that no change is needed (*contra* Hutchinson's *cedit* and Watt's *perdit*). Compare Quintil. *Inst.* 10.1.13: *et 'intellego' et 'sentio' et 'video' saepe idem valent quod 'scio.'*

sensus <labi> : Hutchinson's supplement seems to be the most likely solution (a short disyllabic word is missing in line 124 as well). Compare Verg. *Aen.* 11.818 f.: *labuntur frigida leto* | *lumina, purpureus quondam color ora reliquit*; Statius *Theb.* 8.734 f.: | *ingentesque animos extremo frigore labi* | *sensit...*; Tacit. *Ann.* 6.50: *labi spiritum nec ultra biduum duraturum.*

This is one of the five "slow" lines of the poem, with spondees in the first four feet, along with vv. 5, 52, 114, and 116. If it is deliberately so, the line may well reflect the slow process of Alcestis' dying—φθίνει γὰρ καὶ μαραίνεται νόσῳ (Eurip. *Alc.* 203).

dulcissime coniux | : A common clausula in sepulchral poetry. *dulcissime coniunx* | : *C.L.E.* 542.4; 1139.1; 1338.1; 1436.3. *dulcissima coniunx* | : 708.1; 773.4; 986.9. Cf. *C.I.L.* XI.6417.5: *coniugi dulcissimo.* The sources of the expression are: Catull. 66.33: *pro dulci coniuge* [i.e., Ptolemy III]; Verg. *Aen.* 2.777: | *O dulcis coniunx* [Creusa to Aeneas] = *Alcesta* 118 and 125; *Georg.* 4.465: | *te, dulcis coniunx, te...* [i.e., Eurydice]. Cf. *C.L.E.* 491.4: *dulcis vale, care sodalis.*

123. venit, mors ultima venit : Compare Lucilius Junior ap. Seneca *Epist.* 24.21:

Mors non una *venit*, sed *quae rapit, ultima mors est.*

For such an emotional anaphora compare Eurip. *Alc.* 259 f.: |ἄγει μ' ἄγει τις· ἄγει μέ τις (οὐχ ὁρᾷς;) |νεκύων ἐς αὐλάν; *Alcesta* 161 [= *Aen.* 6.46]: | *"Tempus" ait* [sc. Alcestis]; *"deus, ecce deus!"*; as well as similar emotional anaphoras in the poem (list on p. 13).

124. infernusque deus : As is known, *di inferni* are the θεοὶ
καταχθόνιοι. Compare, e.g., Pacuv. *Trag.* 212; Livy 1.32.10; Lucan
1.634; Juvenal 8.257. In our case, this *infernus deus* is most probably *Dis*,
Pluto: Verg. *Aen.* 6.106: *inferni ianua regis* |; Ovid. *Met.* 2.261: *et infernum
terret cum coniuge regem* |. If *Mors*, of the preceding line, has anything to
do with Euripides' *Thanatos*, then *infernus deus* here may be an echo of
πλησίον "Ἀιδας (Eurip. *Alc.* 268). Contrast *Alcesta* 157 [= *Aen.* 4.258]:
Cyllenia proles, i.e., Mercury is in charge of taking Alcestis to Hades.

claudit <mea> membra sopore | : Compare Lucret. 4.453 f.: *deni-
que cum suavi devinxit membra sopore* | *somnus*; Verg. *Aen.* 8.406: *per membra
soporem* |; Silius 3.170: *mulcentem securo membra sopore* |; *C.L.E.* 481.3: |
Hic iacet aeterno devinctus membra sopore; Seneca *Herc. Oet.* 534: *mortemque
lassis intulit membris sopor* |; Lucan 9.671: *sopor aeternam tracturus morte
quietem*; Propert. 3.11.54: *et trahere occultum membra soporis iter.*

P has *sembra soporem* (for *membra sopore*). This may be reminiscent of
Spanish, *él siembra el sopor*, "he sows slumber."

SUMMARY

The new Alcestis papyrus (copied in 350-400 A.D.) brings us a fascinating late Latin *ethopoeia* consisting of some 124 hexameters, the fruit of a rather ambitious, well-versed, and sophisticated *poeta doctus*. Once restored to its pristine form, the poem displays correct metrics and convincing versification. The Barcelona bard is building upon the best traditions of Latin poetry, and his diction shows unmistakable borrowings from Lucretius, Vergil, Horace, Propertius, Ovid, Tibullus, Seneca, Lucan, Silius, Statius, and popular Latin sepulchral poetry (such as represented by *C.L.E.*). Among the prose writers, Seneca and Pliny are the main sources of inspiration for our poet. What is much more important, he was a very attentive reader of Euripides' *Alcestis*.

The new *Alcestis* consists of twelve "blocks" (or passages), and easily falls into five parts (see p. 4 f.). The main characteristics of its poet seem to be: (1) A carefully conceived design; (2) Mythological and folkloric erudition; (3) Inventiveness and a vivid imagination.

(1) *Design*. It is best reflected in the choice of the term *pietas* (45; 75; 103; *pia* in 78 and 99) to serve as the key-idea of the *ethopoeia*. This term is best understood as deriving from the Euripidean concepts of φιλία ("the bond between the members of a family") and σωφροσύνη ("ethical and religious wisdom"). Accordingly, *pietas* in our poem seems to mean, "the sense of duty of a member (φίλος) within a family." So much so that the expression of 78, *coniux pia*, may well echo Euripides' γυνὴ σώφρων (*Alcestis* 181 f.), both referring to our heroine. Plato's interpretation of Alcestis' φιλία (at *Symposion* 179 c 1) seems to support this suggestion.

The *exemplum pietatis* (103) of the heroine has been successfully pitted against a total lack of this sense of family-duty, on the part of Admetus' father and mother. Much like in Euripides, the Pheres of our poem is a selfish *hedonist*. In her turn, Clymene plays the role of a learned and sophisticated *Stoic philosopher*, who, however, lacks a solid moral foundation. That is why the poet hastens to inform us that Pheres is a πατὴρ ἀπάτωρ (32), and Clymene a μήτηρ ἀμήτωρ (45: *nec pietate, nocens, nec vincitur inproba fletu*).

Admetus is depicted first as a foolish and self-confident ignorant, who wants to learn from his friend Apollo what no mortal man is supposed to know (3-6), and then as a despondent coward (29 and 43), whose endless *crying* resounds throughout his royal palace and the entire poem (22; 24; 44; 45; 71; 107). That is the reason why his brave and noble wife feels that he badly needs encouragement and moral instruction for his future marital life: *Et tu pro coniuge cara | disce mori...!* (102 f.).

The introduction of a rhetorical *Agon* between Clymene (42-70) and Alcestis (71-103) is the most original device of the Barcelona poet. The *rhesis* of each contestant takes about the same length (three "blocks" each), and the *Certamen* itself makes the bulk of the *ethopoeia*. While the Mother displays considerable erudition in adducing religious, philosophical, and mythological arguments to prove her thesis that every man should follow his own destiny (64: *Cur ego de nato doleam, quem fata reposcunt?*), and that therefore a *stellvertretendes Opfer* for her son would only contradict the *Stoic law* of the inevetability of Fate (56), in her turn, the pious Wife has to offer only her *pietas*, her sense of duty as a family-member,—a simple but winning weapon!

The poet has brought the *ethos* of his heroine to its highest peak. Alcestis feels that she has fulfilled her duty in the marriage with Admetus by doing the following. (1) She has married Admetus as a virgin, and borne children to him as her only husband (94). (2) Consequently, she has provided him with the expected heirs, so that her premature death may find no complaint on his part (95). (3) Following the examples of both Euripides' Alcestis and Propertius' Cornelia, our heroine solemnly entrusts her husband with the fruits of their common love (93), while, at the same time, threatening to rise from her grave and come to avenge her crying orphans, in case they are being maltreated by an evil step-mother (98 f.). (4) The pious wife and mother has taken the steps to preserve herself after her death, by leaving behind the children which resemble their mother so much (96 f.).

(5) Above all, Alcestis is happy to offer her life for her husband while serving as a blameless *vicaria victima* for him. Her readiness is reflected in many emotional anaphoras (72; 81 f.), as well as in the expressions, *concedo libens* (73), and *laeta* (110). And her sense of the *reciprocity* of this duty between the spouses in a marriage is best expressed in her slogan: *pro coniuge coniux* (74). (6) Her *pietas* is far-reaching: she has a piece of advice for her husband to serve him for his prospective second marriage: "You too learn to die for your (future) dear wife!" (102 f.). (7) Finally, the noble wife promises to *visit her husband* even from her grave: *Si redeunt umbrae, veniam tecum<que> iacebo* (90). In brief, the Barcelona bard is going out of his way to prove the perfect *pietas* of the heroine of this *ethopoeia*.

(2) *Poeta doctus.* The poem displays a rich repertoire of precious folkloric and mythological motifs. The laurel trees of Apollo Pythius being invoked *along with* the god himself (1 f.). "The tantamount life-

span'' (the transfer of the years of life allotted to one person to the account of another person): *alieno vivere fato* (17; cf. 29 and 73 f.). *Obiectus pectorum* (48), and a mother's womb as a sacred taboo (49 f.). The world-era (*Magnus annus*) of Phoenix (54 f.). The catalogue of the "dying gods" (60-63), and the catalogue of the heroines losing their sons (65-68). After her death, a mother continues to live in the persons of her children provided that they resemble their mother (96 f.). The faithful dead mother avenging her maltreated orphans even from her grave, just as if she came from a *Märchen* of *Brüder Grimm* (98 f.). The motif of the pious heroine *personally* preparing her own funeral pyre (110-116). Last but not least, the motif of the cold *hand of Death* (117 f.).

   (3) *Inventiveness and vivid imagination* (see p. 10 f.). The most significant departure from the traditional myth (as reflected both in Euripides' *Alcestis* 305; 308; 372 f., and in the *Alcesta* of the *Latin Anthology*, 125-28), is in the fact that the Barcelona bard lets his Alcestis entertain the prospect of a second marriage for her husband (in lines 83-85; 98; 102 f.). Most probably, she does so under the influence of Propertius' Cornelia (4.11.85-90). In addition, in his lines 86-88, our poet exploits the *statue-motif* of Alcestis/Laodamia/Cornelia, as found in Euripides (*Alc.* 348-52), Ovid (*Heroid.* 13.151-58), and Propertius (4.11.83 f.). But the point is that his wild imagination had forced him to combine this *effigy-motif* with the strange idea of the shadow of Alcestis coming to *sleep with her living husband* during the night (90: *Si redeunt umbrae, veniam tecum <que> iacebo*). My guess is that the poet stood here under the spell of Propertius' dead Cynthia (4.7.1-6 and 89).

   Finally, it seems more likely than not that, under a similar spell this time of Vergil's Dido (*Aen.* 4.384-86), the imagination of our poet had made his Alcestis *threaten* her husband with the revenge and punishment of an abandoned and forgotten wife, in case he neglected her completely after her self-denying death (100 f.: *Si tibi dissimuler, si...*; the apodosis of the sentence is lost in the lacuna).

   In conclusion, leaving apart the shortcomings common to many late Latin poems (mentioned on p. 13 f.), the new *Alcestis* is a welcome and important acquisition to late Latin poetry.

APPENDIX

THE DATE OF THE POEM

A positive *terminus ante quem* is provided by the script of the Papyrus—second half of the 4th century A.D. A *terminus post quem*, however, is much more difficult to determine. The assumption that the catalogue of "the dying gods" (in lines 60-63) may derive from a Christian apologetic source (cf. p. 53), even if true, can be of little help to us when trying to determine the date of the poem, since such catalogues had become established already around A.D. 200, which is certainly a date too early for our poet on the grounds of his poetic diction, versification, lexicon, syntaxis, and other elements of style.

On the other hand, it seems more likely than not that the Barcelona bard had read Modestinus' captivating and playful epigram about the sleeping Eros, from the *Latin Anthology* (I.1 No. 273 Riese = No. 267 Shackleton Bailey). The text of the epigram, as recently edited by W. D. Lebek (*ZPE* 58 [1985] 37-45), reads as follows:

> Forte iacebat Amor victus puer *alite Somno*   [cf. 104 f.]
> myrti inter frutices *pallentis roris* in herba.   [cf. 113]
> Hunc procul emissae tenebrosa Ditis ab aula
> *circueunt animae*, saeva face quas cruciarat.   [cf. 90]
> 5   "Ecce meus venator!" ait "hunc" Phaedra *"ligemus!"*
>   [cf. 60-63]
>
> "Crudelis crinem" clamabat Scylla *"metamus!"*
> Colchis et orba *Progne* "numerosa caede secemus!"   [cf. 68]
> Sidonis et Canace "saevo gladio *perimamus!*"
> Myrrha "meis ramis Euhadnes igne *crememus!*"
> 10   "Hunc, Arethusa," inquit Byblis "in fonte *necemus!*"
> Ast Amor evigilans dixit: "Mea pinna, *volemus!*"

7 secemus *Lebek* : necemus *codd.* (at *cf.* v.10) || 8 Sidonis *Lebek* : Dido *codd.*

Now, the Barcelona poet seems to share at least five elements with Modestinus' epigram. (1) *A catalogue of tragic heroines*: five of them in our poem (66-68), against no less than ten heroines in Modestinus (5-10). It is true that Procne (*Progne* in both poems) alone appears in both catalogues, but the idea of *dismembering* a living body (either the boy Itys or the boy Eros) is present in both (7: *numerosa caede secemus!*, against line 68 of our poem: *dum colligit ilia cruda*).

(2) An impressive *rhyme-chain*: four rhymes in our poem (60-63), against seven of them in Modestinus (5-11). (3) The expression, *ales Somnus*. As far as I know, it appears only in Modestinus (1) and in our poem (104 f.) in the entire Latin poetry.

(4) In both poems the ghosts of the dead heroines are being allowed to *leave Hades*. Compare Modestinus' line 3 f. (*Hunc procul emissae tenebrosa Ditis ab aula | circueunt animae*) with line 90 of our poem (*Si redeunt umbrae, veniam...*). (5) Finally, there is the similarity between Modestinus' *pallens ros*, "pale dew," [1] (line 2) and *pallida balsama*, "pale myrrh," of our poem (113), both substances being *liquid*.

Even if we leave apart the coincidences (4) and (5) as being less striking, I think the cumulative force of the encounters (1), (2), and (3) is such that the impression our poet had read Modestinus' famous epigram is inevitable. Now, the epigram is tentatively being dated either to the early fourth century (so Norden),[2] or to the late third century A.D. (so Kroll).[3]

In addition, the fourth century A.D. as a probable date for our poem seems to be recommended by other considerations as well. Our poet seems to share with Lactantius and Claudian the interest in the world-era (*Magnus annus*) of the fabulous bird Phoenix: *ubi barbarus ales | nascitur, ac nobis iteratus fingitur orbis* (54 f.). Furthermore, the encounter of our poet with Dracontius seems to be in the expression, *pia pignora* (93, against Dracont. *Romulea* 6.56), in contrast to the expression, *communia pignora* both in Propertius (4.11.73) and Ovid (*Met.* 5.523). In addition, both poets employ the perfect tense, *ivit*, which is rare in poetry (6, against Dracont. *Orestes* 447). Last but not least, the noun *pulver*, employed in neuter gender (as in our line 114), is certainly a late phenomenon, and

---

[1] The second half of line 2 (*pallentis roris in herba*) of Modestinus' epigram I understand as follows: "in the grass (soaked) with pale dew." So did, e.g., Ruhnken, and J. Wight Duff and Arnold M. Duff, in *Minor Latin Poets* (The Loeb Classical Library, 1934), p. 539.

Lebek (o.c., 38-40), however, follows Klotz (1759) in taking *ros* to mean here, *ros marinus*, "rosemary." He refers to Servius ad Verg. *Georg.* 2.213, and translates the line as follows: "zwischen Sträuchern von Myrte im Kraut des bleichen Rosmarins."

This interpretation is not likely to me. Myrtle shrubs and grass make a sufficient bed for the boy Amor: rosemary is not called for. The point is, however, that the expression, "im Kraut des bleichen Rosmarins," seems strained. For grass is one thing, rosemary another, and the combination of grass and rosemary is not convincing.

Consequently, it seems preferable to take the expression, *pallentis roris*, as a *genitivus qualitatis* (or *descriptivus*) to go with *herba*—"in the grass (soaked) with pale dew." Needless to say, grass and dew are brother and sister, and already Ruhnken had referred to Ovid *Fasti* 3.880.

[2] E. Norden, *Die antike Kunstprosa*, 840 n.1: "etwa saec. IV in."

[3] So Teuffel-Kroll-Skutsch, *Geschichte der römischen Literatur*, 6th ed., Leipzig, 1913, III, p. 207.—After Lebek's convincing text of the epigram, Kroll's remark in RE XV (1932) 2321 (s.v. Modestinus 2) is obsolete. Correct is Lebek, o.c., p. 37 n. 1; p. 43 n. 13.

the verb, *disponere* (109), in the sense of "to dispose in a will," seems to hint at the age of the *Vulgate*.

In conclusion, I hope I shall not be far off the mark if suggesting that the Barcelona *Alcestis* was composed probably somewhere around 350 A.D.

One final remark about the possible *place* of our poet. As I have already pointed out (p. 90), the pious Alcestis of our poem personally collects and prepares all the spices and perfumes necessary for her funeral pyre (113: *destringit*; 114: *percidit*; 115: *destringit*). Now, according to the traditional myth, Alcestis lives at the royal *court* of her husband (*castra* = "court," 38) in Pherae, Thessaly. In sharp contrast to this fact, however, the balsam-tree and the cinnamon-tree *do not grow in Thessaly*, but rather throughout the *Near East*. The same is true of the rest of spices and perfumes which our heroine *personally collects* (frankincense, saffron-essence, and amomum). And our poet is well aware of this fact when calling them, "*exotic (eastern) plants and spices*" (112: *barbaricas frondes <et> odores*).

The conclusion that our poet is transferring his heroine from Pherae to somewhere in the *Near East*, where she can personally collect all these spices and perfumes (113-115), I think cannot be avoided. My guess is that the poet wanted to bring his heroine as close *to his own audience* as possible. But the point is that, by so doing, he is inadvertently revealing the region of *his own residence*. Now, in view of the provenance of the Barcelona papyrus, *Egypt* seems to be the best candidate for such a residence. After all, *Alexandria* is the place where the poet Claudian will be born around 370 A.D.

INDEX VERBORUM

* = vox emendata; < > = vox addenda

flamma : haec ubera flammae | diripiant? 48

fleo : nec toto tempore flebo | 79; | flevit Ityn Progne 68; flentes (natos) 99

fletus : nec vincitur inproba fletu | 45; | coniugis ut... vidit... fletus | 71; et fletibus atria conplet | 22

flos : titulumque novo praecingere flore | 89

frater : | et *fratris Stygii regnum 61

frigus : fatali frigore pressos (pedes) | 120

frons : | barbaricas frondes 112

fugio : fugit illa rogantem | 44; in gremium refugit fugientis imago | 121

fundo : | inque sinus fundit lacrimas 44

funus : conponit in ordine funus | 109; para funera nato | 26; post *funera nostra | 76

gaudeo : | tu tumulis gaudere meis? 48

genetrix 18; genetricis | 42

genitor : 18; 23; | hic genitor, non ut genitor 32; (voc.) *genitor 26 et 29

*gnatus 67 : v. natus

gratus : gratamque relinquere lucem | 14; *grate 33

gremium : | Admeti in *gremium 121; | in gremio cineres nostros... tenere | 87

habeo : *habeat 95

habito : tumulosque *habitassem | 41 *heu 12 et 99

hic : | hoc Parcae docuere nefas, hoc noster Apollo | 27; | hoc tantum... rogo 83; | haec super inproperans 46; haec ubera (acc.) 48

hic (adv.) : | hic genitor 32

homo : | quamvis scire *homini 7

hora : | *Hora [sc. mortis] 117

hostis : hostis mihi lucis, | hostis, nate, patris 50-51

iaceo : veniam tecum<que> iacebo | 90; in coniuge fixa *iacebat | 106; meque puta tecum sub nocte iacere | 86

iacto : | iactat membra toro 22

iam : Acherontis adire | iam prope regna tibi 14; | iam tibi cum... supersit 18; | iam vaga... Nox 104; minimam [sc. vitam] vi tollere vis *iam? | 37

ibi : | illic..., <ibi> 56

idem (masc.) 11

ignis : rogi... ultimus ignis | 49

ilia : dum colligit *ilia cruda | [sc. Progne] 68

ille : | ille larem... petit 21; | edocet ille patrem 25; fugit illa rogantem | 44

illic : | illic.., <ibi> 56

imago : mea dulcis imago | 100; refugit fugientis imago | 121

in (cum acc.) : animus quando ivit in auras | 6; in se convertere casus | 16; | inque sinus fundit lacrimas 44; | Admeti in gremium refugit 121.—(cum abl.) : terrena <in> sede morari | 52; | in gremio cineres nostros... tenere | 87; in coniuge fixa iacebat | 106; conponit in ordine funus | 109

indignor : manus *indignanda novercae | 98

infernus : | *infernusque deus 124

Ino : dea perdidit *Ino | 67

inprobus : nec vincitur inproba [sc. mater] fletu | 45

inpropero : haec super inproperans 46

instans : instantis in se convertere casus | 16

invitus : Apollo | invitus... edocuit 28

invoco : | invoco te [sc. Apollinem] 2

ipse : | ipse pater mundi 60

iste : mors ista placet 81; mors ista querellas | 95; (vestigia ne mea) ista legat 85

itero : nobis *iteratus fingitur orbis | 55

Itys : | flevit *Ityn Progne 68

iubeo : | plangere saepe iubet sese 108; iussi<que> idem 11

iubilum : dare iubila silvis | 11

labor : labuntur 69; | ut vidit sensus <labi> 122

lacrima : lacrimis <quae> causa requirit | 24; | inque sinus fundit *lacrimas 44; lacrimasq<ue> viri... videbat | 107

lacrimosus : lacrimosa recedat | vita procul 80

laetus : | laeta [sc. Alcestis] 110

lar : | ille larem... petit 21

lateo : | illic, nate, late 56

Latonius : Latonie Delie Paean | 1

Lauripotens 1

laurus : | invoco te laurusque 2

laus : laus magna mei 76

lego : (vestigia ne mea)... *legat 85; laurusque tuo de nomine *lectas | 2

lethum : per<que> vadum *lethi 63

libens : concedo libens 73

locus : ēst terra *locos 59

longe : effuge longe | 53

rigor omnia [sc. membra] corripiebat |
118
orbis : iteratus fingitur *orbis | 55
ordo : conponit in ordine funus | 109
orior : nox oritur 58

Paean : | praescius heu *Paean 12; |
praescie... *Paean | 1
pallidus : pallida *regna | 8; | *pallida...
destringit balsama 113
paratus : variosque pa<ratus> | 110
Parcae : hoc Parcae docuere 27
parens : vinco pietate *parentem [i.e.
patrem] | 75; oblitus mente parentum |
46
pario : uterum... quo te peperi 50
paro : para funera nato | 26
Parthus 54
parvus : parvos (natos) 98
pater : | ipse pater mundi 60; | hostis,
nate, patris 51; | edocet ille patrem 25;
pater (voc.) 28
paveo : famulumque paventem [sc.
Apollinem] | 9
paulum : | paulum ad te veni<at> 101
pectus : et alto | pectore suspirans 24
pecus : pecudumque ducem 10
Pelieïa : vidit *Pelieïa [i.e., Alcestis] fletus
| 71
pello : pulsus 42
per : | per<que> vadum lethi 63
percido : *percidit pulver amomum | 114
perdo : | perdidit Althaea..., dea perdidit
Ino | 67
pereo : | non *pereo 96; ex arte perisse |
62; peritura videbat | 107
perpetuus : | perpetuum nihil est 57
pes : | volvitur ante pedes 43; | algentis-
que pedes [sc. notabat] 120
peto : | ille larem... petit 21; pete 19
pietas : disce exemplum pietatis | 103; |
nec pietate... vincitur 45; vinco pietate
parentem | 75
pignus : commendo tibi pia pignora natos,
| pignora 93-94
pingo : sideribus Nox pingebatur 104;
*pictosque toros 110
pius : | et coniux pia semper ero 78; matris
pia vindicet umbra | 99; pia pignora
natos | 93
placeo : mors ista placet 81
plango : | cur ego non plangam, sicut
planxere priores? | 65; | plangere saepe
iubet sese 108
Porthmeus : nigro velamine *Porthmeus |
82

porto : | me portet melius... Porthmeus |
82 (*paronomasia*)
posco : si lumina poscas | 32
possum : | tu... potes 29 et 47; | tu poteris
17; qui mortis damna subire | possit 16;
| si semper *posses 52
post (adv.) : quid mi post fata relinquant
| 5. (praep). : post crimina divum | 10;
post dicta 21; post mortem 40; post fata
42; post funera nostra | 76; ne post mea
fata | 83
posthac 17
praecingo : titulumque novo praecingere
flore | 89
praescius : | praescius heu Paean 12; |
praescie Lauripotens 1
premo : | mors vicina premit 13; fatali
frigore *pressos (pedes) 120
prior : sicut planxere priores | 65
pro : pro coniuge coniux | 74; et tu pro
coniuge cara | 102; | si pro me mortem
30; pro te qui mortis damna subire |
possit 15; pro te | 19 et 92
procul : lacrimosa recedat | vita procul 81
prodo : ne parvos (natos) manus... nover-
cae | *prodat 99
Progne : | flevit Ityn *Progne 68
prope : Acherontis adire | iam prope
regna tibi 14
propero : | ad mortem properans 106
propinquo : | Hora propinquabat 117
propter : | quam propter 38
prosper : prospera vita 7
puella : lucem raptura puellae | 117
pulver (neutro genere) : percidit pulver
amomum | 114
purpureus : purpureis destringit cinnama
ramis | 115
puto : | me cole, meque puta... iacere | 86

qualiscumque : | qualiscumque tamen [sc.
Alcestis] 91
quamvis : | quamvis scire homini ...
tormentum 7
quando : da noscere, quando | rumpant
Admeti... fila Sorores | 3; animus
quando ivit in auras | 6
quantus : quanta senectae | vita meae
superest 36
-que : 9; 10; 13; 14; 21; 30; 31; 33; 41; 44;
63; 86; 89; 116; 120; 124.—*-que : 2;
19; 118.—<-que> : 11; 49; 54; 63; 90;
107.—fatoque tuo tumuloque 20; natos-
que virumque | 108; pictosque toros
variosque pa<ratus> | 110; tura
crocumque | 112

sit<ne> 8; | si sine lumine *ero 35; |
nil ero 36; | non ero 77; | et coniux pia
semper ero 78; aliquid tamen esse
videbor | 35; ni prospera vita futura
<est> | 7
super (adv.) : | haec super inproperans 46
supersum : superest 37; cum ... supersit |
18
suspiro : alto | pectore suspirans 24
suus : fatorum damna *suorum | 25

talis : ut talis vidit... fletus | 71
tam : tam similes natos 97
tamen : | ede tamen 9; aliquid tamen esse
videbor | 35; | qualiscumque tamen...
91
tantum : | hoc tantum... rogo 83; nec
nomine tantum | 85
tego : quaecumque *tegit caeli vis 70
tempus : nec toto tempore flebo | 79; si
tempora dones | 29; ego tempora dono
| 73
teneo : cineres nostros dignare *tenere |
87
terra : non<ne> ēst terra locos ...? 59
terrenus : *terrena <in> sede morari |
52
timidus : | nec timida tractare manu 88
Titan : *Titanum ex arte perisse | [sc.
Bacchum] 62
titulus : titulumque novo praecingere flore
| 89
tollo : vi tollere vis iam? | 37
tormentum : | quamvis scire homini... |
tormentum 8
torus : | iactat membra toro 22; pictosque
toros 110
totus : toto tempore 79; totis narrabitur
annis | 77
tracto : | nec timida tractare manu 88; |
*tractavitque manu [sc. Hora mortis]
118
trado : | me, <me> trade neci 72; me
trade sepulcris | 72 et 81
tribuo : (manum) tribuam 34
tristis : | ad natum... *tristem 23; | non
*tristior atros | aspiciam vultus 78
tu : | tu poteris posthac 17; | tu, genitor,
tu, sancte 29; quam [sc. vitam] tu si red-
dere velles | 40; | tu, scelerate, potes...?
47; | tu tumulis gaudere meis? 48; Et tu,
nec nomine tantum | 85; Et tu pro con-
iuge cara | 102.—tibi : Acherontis adire
| iam prope regna tibi 14; | iam tibi
cum genitor... supersit | 18; mea regna
dedi tibi 38; | nate, *tibi concessissem

41; ego tempora dono | ... eventura tibi
74; ne... | dulcior ulla [sc. mulier] tibi
84; commendo tibi pia pignora natos |
93; | si tibi dissimuler...100.—te (acc.)
: | invoco te 2; si te colui 9; (uterum),
quo te peperi 50; <ibi> te tua fata
sequentur | 56; (si non) | paulum ad *te
veniat 101.—te (abl.) : ne deserar a te |
91; solo de te fecunda 94; | ex te sic
nullas habeat... querellas | 95; pro te
qui mortis damna subire | 15; pete,
lumina pro te | qui claudat 19; quod
vitam desero pro te | 92; tecum 86 et 90
tumulo : (pater mundi) tumulatus abisse |
60
tumulus : tumuloque cremetur | 20; |
contristant *tumuli 39; | tu tumulis
gaudere meis? 48; *tumulosque subire |
30; *tumulosque habitassem | 41
tus : tura crocumque | 112
tuus : *tuo de nomine lectas | [sc. laurus]
2; fatoque tuo tumuloque cremetur | 20;
| dum cineres servabo tuos 80; *tuam
concedere lucem | 31; <ibi> te tua fata
sequentur | 56

uber : haec *ubera flammae | diripiant?
48
ubi : ubi barbarus ales | 54
ullus : ne... | dulcior ulla [sc. mulier] tibi
84
ultimus : rogi... ultimus ignis | 49; venit,
mors ultima venit | 123
umbra : matris pia vindicet umbra | 99; |
si redeunt umbrae 90
unguentum : sudare favillas | *unguento
89
unguis : | caeruleos ungues 119
unus : vita quia dulcius *una | nil mihi 39
ut : | hic genitor, non ut genitor 32; | con-
iugis ut talis vidit... fletus | 71; | ut vidit
sensus <labi> 122
uterus : uterum<que>... ignis | con-
sumat, quo te peperi 49

vadum : | per<que> *vadum lethi 63
vagus : vel vagus aër | 70; | iam vaga...
Nox 104
varius : variosque pa<ratus> | 110
vel : vel vagus aër | 70
velamen : nigro velamine Porthmeus | 82
venio : | sed veniat, pro te qui ... 15; si
non... | paulum ad te *veniat... 101; |
si redeunt umbrae, veniam 90; vēnit,
mors ultima vēnit | 123

WORD FREQUENCY

INDEX OF SCRIBAL ERRORS

Figures refer to verses

mestum : maestus 21
parce : Parcae 27
senecte : senectae 36
alpea : Althaea 67
precingere : praecingere 89
umbre : umbrae 90
quecumque : quaecumque 70
leta : laeta 110
ceruleos : caeruleos 119
e for i (cf. *i for e*)
  me : mi 5
  requeret : requirit 24
  fratre : fratri<s> 61
  perdedit... perdedit : perdidit... perdidit
    67
  etin : Ityn 68
  meor : m<or>ior 76
  moreor : morior 96
  rapeor : rapior 123
  claudet : claudit 124
e for o (cf. *o for e*)
  -que : quo 54
-em for -e (cf. *quem for -que* 2)
  pietatem : pietate 45
  acatem : Agaue 66
  soporem : sopore 124
-em for -es
  omnem : omnes 93
-em for -is (cf. *-is for -em*)
  alcestem : Alcestis 107
et for dum 68 (cf. *aut for dum* 80)
-et for -eat
  habet : habe<a>t 95
ex for de (cf. *de for ex*)
  disce ex m<e> : de m<e> disce 103

f for s (cf. *s for f*)
  fi : si 40

g for s
  degero : desero 92

Haplography
  me : me, <me> 72
  quiri : q<ue> viri 107
Heavy Corruption
  itam : <T>ita<nu>m 62
  illa cruentus : ilia cruda 68
  legit illius : tegit <ca>eli v<i>s 70
  niquid : neci 72
  proderentet : prodat, et <h>eu
    (< prodet et en) 99
  † -ones † 111

i for a (cf. *a for i*)
  futuri : futura 7

i for ae (cf. *i for e*)
  piant : Paean 1
  pian : Paean 12
  illi : <ca>eli 70
i for e (cf. *e for i*)
  uellis : velles 40
  ubira : ubera 48
  possis : posses 52
  niquid : neci 72
  digna retinere : dignare 'tenere 87
  alis : ales 104
i for o (cf. *o for i*)
  prigne : Progne 68
i for u
  dissimiles : dissimuler 100
-i for -um (cf. *-um for -i*)
  amomi : amomum 114
i for y
  etin : Ityn 68
Improvisation (cf. *Assimilation*)
  doli piant : Deli<e> P<a>ean 1
  relinqua[[nt]]m : relinquant 5
  uita futuri : vita futura 7
  si {non} te colui 9
  subiret : subire 15
  lacrimarum causa : lacrimis <quae>
    causa 24
  fatorum damna sororum : fatorum
    damna suorum 25 [cf. v. 4]
  ecce uides : ecce, dies, 26
  tuo : tuam 31
  nihil : nil 36 et 40
  sicut suum : si qu<o>d sum 36
  dulcior ullam : dulcius una 39 [cf. v. 84:
    dulcior ulla]
  di[[u]]`e´m : diem 42
  `u´d`u´landus : blandus (*voluit* adu-
    landus?) 43
  aeternam sede : terrena <in> sede 52
  adque (i.e., atque) : ac 55
  multatus : mutatus 61
  diomedes : Diomede 66
  acatem (i.e., Achatem) : Agaue 66
  ion : Ino 67
  et in : Ityn 68
  illa cruentus (*voluit* cruentum) : ilia
    cruda 68
  precedunt : cedunt 69
  illius : <ca>eli v<i>s 70
  peleide : Pelieïa 71
  inquid 72 *et* exclamans 73 : {inquid} *et*
    exclamat (cf. v. 123)
  aut (< aum) : dum 80
  recedam : recedat 80 (cf. v. 5)
  me tradere pulcris : me trade sepulcris
    81

-d

  qui : qui<d> 5
  se : se<d> 28

e

  doli : Deli<e> 1
  lumine <e>ro 35
  Admete <e>ventura 74
  mexempla : m<e> exemplum 103

g-

  <g>natum 67

h

  <h>eu 12 et 99
  aceronis : Ac<h>eron<t>is 13
  abitasse : <h>abitasse<m> 41
  Part<h>us 54
  Bacc<h>um 62
  alpea : Alt<ha>ea 67
  potneus : Po<r>t<h>meus 82
  <H>ora 117

i

  us : v<i>s 37 et 70
  tomul : tumul<i> 39

l

  failas : fa<v>il<l>as 88

-m

  triste : triste<m> 23
  abitasse : <h>abitasse<m> 41
  materna : materna<m> 47
  morte : morte<m> 47

n

  deripiat : diripia<n>t 49

o

  sicut : si qu<o>d 36

p

  ra<p>tura 117

r

  fatebo<r> 12
  digneos : digne<r>is 31
  contustant : cont<r>istant 39
  potneus : Po<r>t<h>meus 82
  desere : desera<r> 91

-s

  siderea<s> 6
  metui<s> 53
  fratre stygium : fratri<s> Stygii 61

t

  aceronis : Ac<h>eron<t>is 13
  itam : <T>ita<nu>m 62

u

  man<u>s 98

v

  failas : fa<v>il<l>as 88

Omission of one syllable

  futura <est> 7
  sit<ne> 8
  <quae> 24

tae : <vi>ta 39
ter<r>ena <in> sede 52
non<ne> 59
<T>ita<nu>m 62
me, <me> 72
m<or>ior 76
indigna<nda> 98
veni<at> 101
conplebent : conpleve<ra>t 105
frondes <et> odores 112

Omission of -que

  11; 49; 54; 63; 90
  -q<ue> 107

Omission of two syllables

  <ibi> 56
  pa<ratus> 110
  <labi> 122
  <mea> 124

-or for -us

  dulcior : dulcius 39

-os for -is (cf. *-is for -os*)

  oculos : oculis 119

-os for -o

  natos : nato 31

-os for -u (cf. *-us for -u*)

  manos : manu 118

p- for -b

  pallada... palsama : pallida ...balsama
  113

p for th

  alpea : Althaea 67

q for c (cf. *c for q*)

  pe[[q]]˙c′udum 10
  qum... qum : cum... cum 18
  doqere : docuere 27
  quicui : cui 53
  niquid : neci 72
  quae for -que 91 et 118
  quae for qui 20
  quam for quia 39
  quem for quam 38
  quem for -que 2
  qui for quid 5
  quid for quod 92
  quod for quo 50

r for s (cf. *s for r*)

  tradere pulcris : trade sepulcris 81

r for t

  proderent et : prodat et <h>eu 99 (?)

s for c

  sur : cur 53

-us for -o (cf. -um for -o)
  tuus : tuo 2
-us for -os
  tumulus : tumulos 41
  locus : locos 59
  atrus : atros 78
  pictus : pictos 110
  arsurus : arsuros 116

-us for -u (cf. -os for -u)
  fletus : fletu 45
-us for -um (cf. -um for -us)
  cruentus : *voluit* cruentum 68

v for n (cf. *n for u*)
  inferuus : infernus 124

INDEX OF VERSE-END CORRUPTIONS

INDEX OF VERSE-END BORROWINGS